JOSEPH COTTON WIGRAM

To friends
Christopher Guiness, Barry Kissell, Richard Kew, Gordon Ogilvie, Paul Rayner, John Simons, Nigel Walker, Tim Watson

Joseph Cotton Wigram

Bishop of Rochester

Educator, Strategist, Pastor and Leader

Nigel Scotland

GRACEWING

First published in England in 2021
by
Gracewing
2 Southern Avenue
Leominster
Herefordshire HR6 0QF
United Kingdom
www.gracewing.co.uk

All rights reserved

No part of this publication may be reproduced,
stored in a retrieval system, or transmitted in any
form or by any means, electronic, mechanical,
photocopying, recording or otherwise,
without the written permission of the publisher.

© 2021, Nigel Scotland

The rights of Nigel Scotland to be identified as the author
of this work have been asserted in accordance
with the Copyright, Designs and Patents Act 1988.

The publishers have no responsibility
for the persistence or accuracy of URLs for websites
referred to in this publication, and do not guarantee
that any content on such websites is, or will remain,
accurate or appropriate.

ISBN 978 085244 964 6

Cover picture: Joseph Cotton Wigram,
watercolour after Sir George Richmond.
Courtesy of the late Canon Sir Clifford Wigram Bart.

Typeset by Word and Page, Chester, UK

Cover design by Bernardita Peña Hurtado

Contents

Foreword	vii
Preface	xi
Acknowledgements	xiii
List of Abbreviations	xiv
1. Early Days in Essex	1
2. St James's, Westminster, and the National Society	7
3. East Tisted Rectory and Archdeacon of Winchester	27
4. Rector of St Mary's, Southampton	43
5. Bishop of Rochester	61
6. Doubts, Ritualism and Bishop Colenso	87
7. Pastor of the Clergy and People	109
8. Evangelical Convictions	127
9. Joseph Cotton Wigram, A Significant Leader	139
Bibliography	151
Index	157

Foreword

To be asked to write this Foreword has been to me both a pleasure and a surprise. It is a pleasure because I am a longstanding admirer of Nigel Scotland's historical scholarship, and the enormous energy he has invested not only in getting English church history right, but, more interestingly, in filling gaps, exploring side paths and portraying little-known characters whom the standard historians have missed. Filling a gap, for instance, was exemplified in his biography of John Sumner, Archbishop of Canterbury from 1848 to 1862. Every successor of Sumner to the present day became the subject of a biography within 30 years of his death (recent ones while still alive); Sumner, the first evangelical since the sixteenth century to come to Canterbury, languished with little about him accessible to the average reader. But Nigel Scotland filled that gap, and I for one greatly appreciated being able to add Sumner to my shelves and my grasp of nineteenth-century church history. This present biography falls more into the category of portraying a little-known character (and I return to Wigram himself below), and it enables the author to draw upon his previous studies in the nineteenth century (clearly his favourite arena), and to engage his talents in the microscopic enquiries proper to such a biography; so for Wigram here are detailed family records, quotations from letters to clergy, cuttings from local papers, and a host of *minutiae* such as to give colour and three-dimensional credibility to this bishop from nearly two hundred years ago.

I knew Nigel Scotland as a student 55 years ago. He was an evangelical from a constituency which was only just emerging from a ghetto (the famous Keele Congress came during his diaconate), a ghetto which had been marked, *inter alia*, by a paucity of scholarship (look to your books: what literature written by Anglican evangelicals between 1900 and 1950 do you have there?). So here is a writer who, having a recognized gift for scholarship, has for those 55 years given himself to assisting the lagging constituency back into intellectual respectability. Of course he remains an evangelical, and no doubt that impinges on his

Joseph Cotton Wigram

historical interests—but, lest anyone mistake that acknowledgment, I quickly add that no historian is without an angle. This is true not only of Lytton Strachey or Humphrey Carpenter; even an Owen Chadwick has a basis for his selection of material. The test is not whether the author has a faith and a theological position of his own (and Nigel Scotland has the integrated position of an evangelical theologian who is also a pastor), but whether there is a sympathetic presentation of positions which the author does not hold, and a critical approach to those traditions which the author might have been expected to endorse at sight.

I began by saying that this task gave me not only a pleasure, but also a surprise. How so? Well, I must come clean and admit that Wigram was little more than a name to me, and he is the surprise. I had seven years myself in Rochester diocese and must have heard his name read in the remembrances at the cathedral (he came somewhere after John Fisher and Nicholas Ridley), but I cannot recall much else. I now know much more about how he stood in true succession to Ridley. In both his convictions and his energy in living out and ministering his convictions he mirrors Ridley closely. Born in 1798, he was ordained deacon in 1822, presbyter the year following, and bishop in 1860. So the man and his ministry in whatever capacity, through until he died in 1867, were a considerable (and refreshing) surprise to me. He was a wholly convinced evangelical who yet won the loyalty and trust of the hundreds of clergy of every theological hue within his vast diocese. Apparently an evangelical with warmth and imagination can do that.

I mention his vast diocese. Again, the vastness is something I knew cerebrally—that until 1877 Rochester diocese, while by its name belonging in West Kent, in fact encompassed North of the Thames the whole county of Hertford, almost all of Essex, and a slice of East London. But it is when I follow Wigram's moves on the map that I start to appreciate the scale of it all. Indeed the first decision he had to make was where to live, and the answer he gave himself was Danbury, somewhat to the east of Chelmsford but giving access to much of his far-flung territory! Travel was no new experience for him—he had had thirteen years as Archdeacon of Winchester with the whole of Hampshire and the Isle of Wight as his bailiwick. Thirty years before there would have been no trains and no penny-post and in 1860 he could avail himself of both.

Foreword

Trains apart, transport was horse-drawn. I suppose I had always visualized Bishops of Rochester catching the ferry North from Gravesend, but in fact Wigram, going in the opposite direction, got to Greenwich, Woolwich and Rochester by keeping a house in London and using the trains, in effect going overnight to visit his own diocese, indeed his own cathedral. And in his regular visiting, including a great round of confirmations, he was pioneering, however sketchily, a truly pastoral role towards his parishes. He drew deeply upon the scriptures, gained energy from his love of God and neighbour, and virtually never ceased from his labours.

A pleasure and a surprise; so it will be to all who open it.

Bishop Colin Buchanan
(Assistant Bishop of Rochester 1989–96)

Preface

Lord Palmerston served two terms as Prime Minister—the first from 1855 to 1858 and the second from 1859 to 1865. During these periods in office he appointed thirteen new men to the bench of bishops. In all these appointments he was either prompted or influenced in some way by his step-son-in-law, the 7th Earl of Shaftesbury. A number of nineteenth-century historians, particularly High Churchmen and journalists of the ecclesiastical press, were either critical of or scathing about the appointees. The Bishop of Oxford, Samuel Wilberforce, called them 'wicked insults to the church'[1] and Baring Gould denounced them as 'hempen homespuns'.[2] On the other hand, *The Record* and *Christian Observer* both expressed their gratitude to the Palmerston bishops for upholding the Protestant Reformation and for their pastoral care and diocesan administrative skills. More recent opinion has taken the view that they were good bishops.[3]

Among those appointed by Palmerston during his second ministry was Joseph Cotton Wigram, who was chosen for the See of Rochester. Although dubbed a 'disastrous' appointment[4] by *The Saturday Review* and 'an episcopal blunder'[5] by the *Pall Mall Gazette*, Wigram, who is the subject of this biography, in fact emerges from biased criticism as a significant Christian leader, visionary strategist, dynamic parish minister and an able pastor and diocesan bishop. His life offers a valuable resource to anyone in Christian leadership.

Almost all my life has been spent lecturing and teaching Church and Christian history in a college of higher education, two universities and two theological colleges and this has undoubtedly fuelled my faith and helped to develop my pastoral work. It is indeed regrettable that Church History has a relatively low profile in the theological college and university courses. Many of those being ordained in the Church of England appear to have very little knowledge of the early church or Reformation let alone Victorian or Modern Christianity.

Nigel Scotland
Honorary Research Fellow, University of Gloucestershire
Lecturer, Ripon College, Cuddesdon

Notes

1. Ashwell and Wilberforce 1881, vol. 3, p. 84.
2. S. Baring-Gould 1914, p. 188.
3. See Chadwick 1970, part 1, pp. 468–76, and Scotland 2000.
4. *The Saturday Review*, 29 December 1860.
5. *The Pall Mall Gazette*, 2 December 1860.

Acknowledgements

I should like to acknowledge the kindness of Canon Sir Clifford Wigram who kindly gave me access to letters, notes, and family papers. Mr Gerrard Wigram of Constantia Vale, South Africa, also shared some relevant family details. I am indebted to a number of archivists and librarians who helped me along the way. Josephine Parker at Waltham Forest Archives in the Vestry House Museum helped with documents relating to Walthamstow and Leytonstone. Dr R. J. Palmer at Lambeth Palace Library guided me through the Tait and Golightly correspondence. Dr Mary Clare Martin filled me in on Eleanor Wigram's family home and her charitable activities. I also received help and advice from Diana Chardin, Assistant Keeper of Manuscripts at Trinity College, Cambridge. The archivists at the Hampshire Record Office, the Southampton City Library and Archives and the Essex Record Office all gave me invaluable help, including photocopying many documents and newspaper articles.

I am very grateful to the Revd Dr Alan Munden, who read the manuscript and gave helpful advice. The Revd Dr Paul Roberts, Lecturer in Church History at Trinity College, Bristol, and Bishop Nazir Ali, who was Bishop of Rochester from 1994 to 2004, have both kindly endorsed my text. Finally, I owe a special debt to Bishop Colin Buchanan, who first introduced me to Church history and taught me when I was a student at the London College of Divinity: I am honoured by his very generous Foreword.

Abbreviations

Libraries and record offices referred to in the references

CWAC	City of Westminster Archives Centre, 10 St Ann's Street, London SW1
HRO	Hampshire Record Office, Sussex Street, Winchester
CERC	Church of England Record Centre, Lambeth Palace
LPL	Lambeth Palace Library, London SE1 7JU
NSA	Archives of the National Society, Church of England Record Centre, Lambeth Palace
SCA	Southampton City Archives, 140 Above Bar Street, Southampton
WFA	Waltham Forest Archives and Local History Library, Vestry House Museum, Walthamstow, London E17 9NH

1

Early Days in Essex

Born on 26 December 1798 at Walthamstow House,[1] Joseph Cotton Wigram was the sixth son[2] of Sir Robert Wigram (1744–1830) and his second wife, Eleanor (1767–1841), by whom he had thirteen sons and four daughters.* Sir Robert was one of the greatest business men of his time.† Having first trained in medicine he served as a surgeon on a number of ships, several of which were bound for India. By 1788 he had saved sufficient capital to purchase a ship of his own. This was the celebrated *General Goddard*, a 755-ton East Indiaman, which was regularly chartered by the East India Company. Wigram then commissioned the building of a new vessel, the *True Briton*, and the stage was set for the making of a large fortune. By 1813 he was the owner of twenty ships. In addition, he acquired a controlling interest in the Blackwall ship-building yard, became chairman of the new East India Docks Company in 1810, head of Huldart's Rope Works and a partner in Reid's Brewery. He also built alms-houses and schools in Poplar and erected Green's

---

* By his first wife Catherine Broadhurst (d. 1787) Robert had six children.

† Robert's father, John Wigram, was born in 1712 and came from Wexford. Comparatively little is known of him apart from the fact that he was a sailor and a commander of a privateer called *The Boyne*. In 1742 he set sail from Bristol bound for Malaga but was forced by stormy weather to put in at Wexford. There he spent time with his cousin Mary Clifford, whom he married. Robert, who was born on 30 January 1744, never saw his father, who was lost at sea, and he was brought up by his uncle and his mother. Robert Wigram arrived in London in 1762 with £200 in his pocket and a letter from his mother to a Dr Allen with a request that he should be taught medicine. Robert duly trained and served as a surgeon on a number of ships. With the passage of time he has sufficient money to purchase a ship of his own. From this beginning he eventually became a major ship owner and East India Company trader, see Lubbock 1924, pp. 37–41.

Joseph Cotton Wigram

Sailors Home in East India Dock Road.[3] He enjoyed a warm and close relationship with his second wife, Eleanor and said of her, 'I never did undertake any business of moment without consultation with my wife, and can truly say it has much promoted my fortune'.[4]

In addition to all of these activities Sir Robert was elected to Parliament as the member for the little Cornish seaport of Fowey in 1802. He was a strong supporter of Prime Minister William Pitt and became Vice-President of the Pitt Club. In the General Election of 1806 he was elected as the member for Wexford, the Irish town in which he was born. However, the following year he retired both from office and public life and was made a Baronet and High Sheriff of Essex. He lived out his later years doubtless enjoying his large estate and the gracious environment of Walthamstow House, which he had purchased about the year 1782.[5] Sir Robert was hugely wealthy and before he died he made handsome provision for each of his sons as well as leaving his second wife his house, estate and an income of about £5,000 a year.[6]

Sir Robert had a large family totalling twenty-three children, who were devoted to him. Once a year he would gather the whole family together, get a bundle of twenty-three faggots and show how they could not be broken. Whenever there was a birth in his family he showed his gratitude by 'releasing a prisoner confined for debt by paying up for him'.[7] In 1857 sixteen of the family met and their ages totalled a thousand years.

Since his childhood days Robert Wigram had a heart for the poor and in his later years always treated his servants well. Nanny Pearce was nurse to the family for forty-eight years and brought up all twenty-three children. A monument was erected in honour of her service in Walthamstow church. Alice Escott, his housekeeper, stayed with him for forty-one years and was buried at St Helen's, Bishopsgate.

From these vignettes it is plainly obvious that the Wigrams were a prominent and wealthy family. Sir Robert and his wife were clearly loving, kind and compassionate people. Joseph Cotton was brought up in a caring environment of plenty in which one can imagine that no expense was spared. He was baptised Joseph Cotton on 1 April 1799,[8] his Christian names being chosen as a compliment to his father's close friend and business partner, Joseph Cotton (1746–1825).[9] Significantly in later years Joseph Cotton's son, William, prospered in business and became one of the governors of the Bank of England. He seems also to have been a friend and associate of Joseph Cotton Wigram. From 1819 he lived with his wife and family in Leytonstone, where the Wigrams also resided and where Joseph was curate from 1822 to 1827. William Cotton played a major role in the building of a new church in Stepney, variously known as Stepney Chapel and Stepney New Church and later as St Philip's. Subsequently he took an active part in the London Diocesan Church Building Society. He was one of the founders of the National Society in 1811, formed for establishing schools grounded on the principles of the Church of England—the Liturgy and teaching based on the Prayer Book and the Catechism. Joseph Wigram was later to become the Society's General Secretary. Cotton also shared Wigram's commitment to the work of the Society for the Propagation of the Gospel in Foreign Parts.[10]

Sir Robert Wigram was clearly a man of faith, who was a Vice-President of the South West Bible Society Auxiliary[11] and a known and frequent subscriber to several evangelical societies.[12] He was concerned that his children should grow up in the Christian faith. In a private letter to his second wife Eleanor, dated 1 April 1820, he wrote: 'My children have my fullest affection. Assure them that to be good is to be happy, and get them to read that favourite sermon of mine,—we love him because he loved us—and another—draw nigh unto God, and He will draw nigh to you.'[13] Lady Wigram was clearly a devoted and active Christian. Wigram's descendant, Clifford Wigram, described her as 'a staunch Christian Woman'.[14] In 1815 she founded the Walthamstow Female Benefit Society, of which she became the patroness and sole treasurer.[15] She exerted a dominant influence on other voluntary associations in the Anglican Church,[16] and in 1824 she founded the Ladies' Auxiliary of the Church Missionary Society, which rapidly became more successful than the male-run branch.[17]

EDUCATION

Joseph Cotton received some education at home and attended a private school in Fulham.[18] He was educated by private tutors and proceeded

Joseph Cotton Wigram

to Trinity College, Cambridge. He graduated BA in 1820 and MA in 1823. It is not certain exactly how Wigram came to his strong evangelical faith but he was a resident undergraduate at Trinity, Cambridge, at the time when Simeon's ministry at was at its height and impacting many students. Charles Simeon (1759–1836) was the leader of the Evangelical Revival in the Church of England. Educated at Eton and King's College, Cambridge (where in 1782 he was elected a Fellow), Simeon was ordained priest in 1783 and in the same year he was appointed Vicar of Holy Trinity Church, a post he held until his death. In his early days he met with considerable hostility from both the university and his congregation. But his pastoral care gradually overcame the opposition and he came to exercise a considerable influence among the undergraduates and ordinands. He also became a leading figure in the Missionary movement and was one of the founders of the Church Missionary Society in 1799. The East India Company often consulted him over its choice of chaplains. It is hard to imagine that the young Wigram would not have come under this influence during his time at Cambridge. Arthur Young included Trinity as 'one of the colleges from which "Simeonites" went out to spread the evangelical Gospel at its most characteristic over England and exert their influence on the morals of the English people'.[19]

ORDINATION AND EARLY MINISTRY

Wigram was ordained deacon by the Bishop of Ely in the chapel of the bishop's palace on 3 November 1822 to serve the curacy of Leytonstone in south Essex. He was ordained priest on Trinity Sunday the following year on 25 May 1823 by William Howley, the Bishop of London. At this time Leytonstone was described as 'a straggling village, about six miles from London upon Epping road'. It was a chapelry in the parish of Leyton, which was opened for use in April 1749 and later enlarged and re-opened on the 23 January 1820.[20] The area around the church contained the country residences of many of the wealthy commercial inhabitants of London. The incumbent under whom Wigram served was Charles Henry Laprimaudaye, who had been instituted to the vicar-

Early Days in Essex

age of Leyton by Beilby Porteous, Bishop of London, on 22 March 1800. Laprimaudaye remained in post until his death at the age of 85 in 1848.*

Not many details have survived of these early years of Wigram's ministry but one can well imagine he was conscientious in his pastoral care and preaching. There are details of baptisms and marriages which he performed recorded in the registers of St Mary's. Sometimes he signs himself as 'officiating minister' and at others as 'Curate of Leytonstone'.[21] Wigram's ministry was clearly effective and prospered because in 1829 the chapel was found to be 'far too small for the needs of the area and a subscription list was opened for the building of a proper church'.[22] Generous support, doubtless from the pockets of the many wealthy local inhabitants, was quickly forthcoming and building commenced in 1832 on a new site purchased and donated by William Cotton of Walwood House, who had been one of the prime movers behind the project.[23] In 1845 the new chapel became St John's Church, Leytonstone.

After four and a half years in Leyton Wigram left to become assistant preacher at St James's, Westminster, usually called St James's, Piccadilly. His ministry in London proved to be hugely demanding both in time and energy.

Notes

1. WFA, St Mary's Leyton, Baptismal Register, 1 April 1799.
2. See *The Family of Wigram*, privately printed pamphlet in the possession of Canon Sir Clifford Wigram Bt.
3. Savell 1964, p. 30.
4. H. Green and R. Wigram, *Chronicles of Blackwall Yard*, part I (London: 1881), p. 54.
5. R. S. Wigram, *Biographical Notes*, 1912, p. 19.
6. Lubbock 1924, p. 44.
7. *Ibid.*, p. 38.
8. WFA, St Mary's Leyton, Baptismal Register, 1 April 1799.

* Of Huguenot descent, Laprimaudaye had graduated MA from Christ Church, Oxford. He was a member of British Association for the Advancement of Science and of the Oxford Society for the Study of Gothic Architecture. During his incumbency he added a south aisle and a vestry at St Mary's. His nephew, the Revd Charles John Laprimaudaye, was also an Anglican clergyman, before converting to Catholicism. Savell 1964, p. 31.

Joseph Cotton Wigram

9 *Dictionary of National Biography.*
10 *Ibid.*
11 Brown 1961, p. 247.
12 *Ibid.*, p. 357.
13 R. Wigram, letter to Lady Wigram, 1 April 1820, in R. S. Wigram, *Biographical Notes*, 1912.
14 C. Wigram, letter to Nigel Scotland, 12 December 1995.
15 Martin 1995, p. 126.
16 *Ibid.*
17 *Ibid.*, p. 127.
18 Venn 1954, p. 461 (entry for Joseph Cotton Wigram).
19 Brown 1961, p. 295.
20 WFA, Brenn and Kennedy, 'History of Leyton', vol. 6, p. 55.
21 WFA, see St Mary's Leyton, Baptismal Register, entries 7 September 1823, 26 February 1826 and 30 November 1826; and Marriage Register, entries 279, 30 April 1823 and 379, 30 April 1826.
22 Savell 1964, p. 30.
23 *Ibid.*, p. 31.

2

St James's, Westminster, and the National Society

At the time of Wigram's arrival, the parish of St James, Westminster, was under the direction of the rector, John Gifford Ward, who had been instituted to the living by the Bishop of London in 1825. Ward was later to become Dean of Lincoln in 1845.[1] The parish also included a chapel-of-ease, which dated back to 1686, for which the incumbent and clergy were responsible. Towards the end of his time at Westminster Ward was attracted to some of the practices which were being adopted by the ritualists. When he began to preach wearing a surplice, the parish clerk recorded that there was 'so much opposition that the black gown was resumed'.[2] There is, however, nothing to suggest that during his time in the parish Wigram's relations with Ward were anything other than cordial.

The parish of St James was one of great contrasts. The main church of St James attracted the wealthy and prosperous having its 1827 church rate assessed at £2,560 14s. 5¾d.[3] while the chapel of St Luke, Berwick Street, which stood in the poorest area, was computed at the lesser sum of £1,445 10s. 1d.[4] Many of the London nobility were pew holders at St James, among them Lady Beauchamp, who paid £12 10s. a year for the privilege, the Duke of Bedford, who was assessed at £9 9s., and Earl Spencer, who was charged £10 6s.[5] It may be that Wigram's frequent presence at Sunday worship in St James brought him to the notice of the Duke of Clarence. Whether this was so or not Wigram carried the title of 'Domestic Chaplain to his Royal Highness the Duke of Clarence' when on 11 June 1827 he preached a sermon, which was subsequently published.[6]

The parish was listed in the 1831 census as having 37,051 inhabitants. They were composed of 8,344 families, 5,575 of which were engaged in trades. The greater part of their number were crowded together 'in the most wretched manner' on the eastern side of the parish towards Soho and St Giles. Wigram noted that 'the vast majority of them lived 'in single badly ventilated rooms, from six to twelve families in a house, the house highly rented, and commonly managed by landlords who hold a set of such houses for no other purpose than that of gain'. He also recorded the people's 'distress from the fluctuations of trade, and their temptations from the surrounding iniquity, which were indeed often great'.[7]

Wigram recounted that the parish was divided into six districts, under six resident clergymen. Each of the districts were then further subdivided into sixty smaller parts in order to visit the poor and distribute charitable aid especially in times of distress, extreme cold or prevailing sickness. 'This division of work', Wigram observed, 'was the secret of such strength as we had.'[8] The particular district for which he was responsible contained 660 houses with above 2000 families. For them he devised his own strategy, which consisted of calling on parents of children in the schools, calling on those who rented pews in the church, visiting in their homes those parents whose children he had baptised or had been confirmed and taking particular care for bereaved families. The baptism and marriage registers indicate the demanding nature of Wigram's assignment. In just the months of June and July 1828 he performed a hundred and twenty baptisms.[9] In the year 1830 he officiated at a hundred and ten marriages. In addition, another curate, Murray Browne, was responsible for a similar number of wedding services. In contrast the rector, J. G. Ward, seems to have enjoyed a quieter life officiating at less than a half-a-dozen weddings in 1830.[10] Among those who brought their children for baptism were coachmen, tailors, bricklayers, shopkeepers, servants, labourers and shoemakers.[11] If any of their number ever ventured out to church services it would probably have been to the chapel-of-ease.

The social environment and the physical conditions of the parish were challenging. The Thames had become heavily polluted with discharge from the sewers that caused drinking water to be contaminated.

St James's, Westminster, and the National Society

Preaching in June 1827 Wigram warned, 'Alluvial accumulations are year by year increasing the obstructions of this river to such an extent, that... notwithstanding all efforts its utility will in time be materially impaired, if not wholly destroyed'.[12] This led to a severe outbreak of cholera in parts of the metropolis in 1832. By the end of the following year not only was there widespread sickness, St James's vestry was complaining of the 'uncontrollable turbulence and profligacy of the inhabitants around Peter Street, which deterred "respectable families" from attending the Berwick Street Chapel of Ease'.[13] As well as pastoral visiting Wigram paid particular attention to the parish's five new schools. It was therefore no surprise that in 1834 he was selected to give evidence to a Parliamentary Select Committee on Education. Among other things he stated that visiting societies had now become common. His own visitors went 'ostensibly' to invite the poor to become members of a Provident Society, which could report on sickness or distress and then ensure that their needs could be met. Wigram pointed out that in London in 1828 the General Society for Promoting District Visiting helped such Provident Societies to channel their funds to the poorer parishes.[14]

Wigram did his best to encourage observance of the Lord's Day and gave special addresses to the people generally and sometimes just to gatherings of the trades people. He catechised the children in St Luke's chapel-of-ease and also gave special Advent and Lent addresses. The chapel also had its own lending library. The whole parish had its own Provident Institution, its own Bank for small loans and there was also a coal, clothing and bread club. In the midst of these demanding circumstances Wigram's constant labours and organisational gifts demonstrated that he was an able strategist.

In later years Wigram was able to look back and reflect on the successes of the organisation and strategies which he had helped to put in place in the parish of St James, Westminster. The schools to which particular attention had been paid, multiplied from three with 220 scholars to eight schools with 1,200 scholars. The chapel-of-ease grew from having a congregation of five to eight adults at its afternoon congregation 'to being really well attended' with the Sunday school teachers increasing from twelve to twenty-six. Parish visitors, who were for the most part women, were able to ascertain those who were sick or in need and communicate back to the clergy. The chapel library 'was generally crowded by people borrowing books with 2,600 loans recorded in 1837'.[15] Wigram was particularly thankful that £12,210 had been collected from the people of the parish and that this sum with the aid of public grants had enabled the chapel-of-ease to be rebuilt at a total cost of £14,000. It was opened as St Luke's Berwick Street by the Bishop of London on 23 July 1839.[16]

When Wigram finally left Westminster he did so with positive and good memories. He wrote that he went to London in 1827 'with prejudices on my own mind which I have endeavoured to correct'. He found the people among whom he lived and worked to be 'kindhearted and grateful'.[17]

SECRETARY TO THE NATIONAL SOCIETY

In contrast to the areas close to St Luke's the prosperous area of the parish attracted many of the rich and powerful to its Sunday worship in the main church of St James. And it was doubtless in some measure due to their influence that in June 1827, the year of his arrival in central London, he was appointed secretary to The National Society for Promoting the Education of the Poor in the Principles of the Established Church in England and Wales. It is not clear exactly how this appointment came about but it may have been through the Bishop of London, who rented pew number 42 in the church for the annual sum of £10 6s.[18] Besides the Bishop of London, many of the city's good and the great worshipped at St James and may also have commended their new assistant preacher for the role. Among those listed as renting pews were Lord Rosslyn (and those members of the nobility mentioned on page 7) in the North Gallery, and the Duke of Buckingham, Lord George Cavendish and the Earl of Hardwick 'on the North Wall'.[19] Another factor in Wigram's appointment must have been the fact that both his parents, Sir Robert and Lady Wigram, were prominent members of the National Society. Indeed Sir Robert is listed in the Annual Minutes as having subscribed ten guineas in both 1828[20] and 1829.[21] Lady Wigram was also listed among the subscribers. It was probably no surprise therefore that the Archbishop of Canterbury himself nominated Wigram for the post. At their meeting held on 13 June 1827 the General Committee resolved unanimously that 'the Rev. Jos. C. Wigram be appointed'.[22]

London life and ministry in Westminster must have been both demanding and stressful, to say the least, for Wigram, who had to combine parochial work with his National Society responsibilities. Then there was the added role at St James, since the clergy were also responsible for services and pastoral care of St Luke's, Berwick Street.[23]

MARRIAGE

During his time at Westminster Joseph Cotton married Susan Maria Arkwright on the 1 March 1837. Their marriage took place at Wirksworth in Derbyshire and was conducted by the bride's uncle the Revd Joseph Arkwright. Susan, who was born on 11 February 1812 and died on 27 June 1864, was the second daughter of Peter Arkwright, Esq, of Rockford House, Cromford, a grandson of Sir Richard Arkwright, the inventor of the spinning frame and one of the pioneers of the Industrial Revolution in Britain.[24] There were several close links between the Wigram and the Arkwright families. Peter Arkwright's brother, the Revd Joseph Arkwright, (1791–1864) had married Anne Wigram in 1818[25] and his sister Anne Arkwright (1794–1844) married Sir James Wigram in the same year. Joseph and Susan's first child Susan Caroline was born in 1838. They went on to have ten children in total, seven boys and three girls.[26]

Wigram's first occasion as secretary of the National Society took place at the General Committee Meeting held St Martin's Vestry Room on 13 June 1827. It was noted that the Archbishop of Canterbury had been pleased to nominate him 'as a gentleman well qualified to fill the office of secretary'.[27] Besides taking the minutes of the meetings Wigram's commitments were many and varied. There were mundane issues such visiting incumbents who had responsibility for church schools, checking whether schools who applied to the society for grants were genuinely educating the poor as the society required, ascertaining if schools were using books which were not in the society's approved list and liaising with the Society's solicitor on legal matters. Thus at the General Committee Meeting held in December 1830 Wigram was required to inform the incumbent of Criccieth and Bangor that his parochial school must be educating the poor before a grant could be made.[28] In April the following year he informed the Committee of the results of their survey, which showed that 133 schools in the National Union were using books not listed in the catalogue of The Society for the Promotion of Christian Knowledge.[29]

Wigram did not confine his role as secretary to the Society to a purely administrative one. In his ministry in Westminster and Berwick Street he was daily made aware of the practical educational needs of the poor. In 1832 he published *Elementary Arithmetic, for the Information of the Masters and Mistresses of National Schools*, which became widely used. It was noticed, somewhat grudgingly, by *The Morning Chronicle*, on account of Wigram's position with the Society, 'the work, therefore, demands more attention from us than it would otherwise deserve ... A work, therefore, by the Revd J. C. Wigram, connected with education, may be regarded as a semi-official document put forth by the National Society'.[30] One of his particular concerns was to try and make children aware of the historical reality of the Christianity while at the same time as helping them to have a personal faith of their own. In 1832 and 1833 he published two more books in an endeavour to respond to these needs.

The first of these two volumes was *The Geography of the Holy Land intended to serve as an Explanatory key to the Map of Palestine: with a copious index.*[31] This small cloth-bound volume of one hundred and sixty pages went through several editions. In his preface Wigram stated that important doctrines are associated with the names and places of Israel. 'Nothing', he wrote, 'will illustrate better the history of our Lord, or fix it more deeply on the memory, than the giving, as it were, a plan of those places where particulars of his life occurred.'[32] The book's chapters cover a general description of the Holy Land including mountains, rivers and the people and kingdoms of Israel and Judah. There is a particular focus on the journeys of Jesus and 'the modern conditions of the Holy Land'. Typical of the many sections in the book are Wigram's brief comments on Dalmanutha. 'Our blessed Saviour passed from Sidon to the Eastern side of the Sea of Galilee, Mark vii.31, making a considerable circuit;

and from thence he went over the lake, and came to Magdala. Matt. xx. 39. Mark viii.10.'[33]

In his final chapter on 'The modern condition of the Holy Land' Wigram traced the developments in the nation of Israel from the destruction of Jerusalem in AD 70, through the surrender of the Jews to Muhammad in AD 637 and the medieval crusades, down to the overrunning of the land by the Ottoman Turks in 1516. He followed with an examination of Moses' prophecies concerning Israel in the Book of Deuteronomy and concluded,

> And what nation has ever suffered so much or so long. Who shall not confess, that the miseries they have endured have rendered them A SIGN AND A WONDER FOR EVER TO THE WORLD. Deut. xxviii. 46. Well then! Let everyone that reads understand the warning of St Paul, BECAUSE OF UNBELIEF, THEY [LIKE BRANCHES] WERE BROKEN OFF, AND THOU STANDEST BY FAITH! BE NOT HIGH MINDED, BUT FEAR! Rom. XI. 20.[34]

In this reference to Israel we see Wigram was among those Evangelicals who believed that the Jews had unique role in the coming millennium and the last times. His concluding chapter must have been written for the benefit of teachers for the complexities of his eschatology were well beyond the grasp of child labourers and farm workers.

The year following Wigram published *Practical Hints on the Formation and Management of Sunday-Schools*.[35] This was an extremely practical handbook, which also went through several editions. It was written for the clergy and people of the upper and middle classes with the aim of persuading them of the crucial need to form Sunday schools, if possible in conjunction with their local parish churches. Whilst Wigram noted the importance of providing schooling for the children of farmers, traders and those running small businesses, his particular concern was the children of the working poor, who in most manufacturing districts were compelled of necessity to leave school at the age of nine or ten. 'The following four or five years', Wigram reminded his readers, is the time in which to strengthen their Christian principles, 'at the momentous period, when, on leaving School, they are first exposed to the temptations awaiting them in the world.'[36] Wigram did not expect every Sunday school to look or function in precisely the same way.

Some might simply meet on Sunday morning and focus primarily on Christian instruction. Others might meet for a two-hour session in both morning and afternoon and include reading and writing as well biblical teaching. Wigram was clear that at the very least every Sunday school should be formed under the patronage of a clergyman, who should, ideally, be the director and work in concert with the superintendent. 'Without the parochial clergyman at the head of it', Wigram's view was, 'it cannot hope to be regarded by the parishioners as an institution for sound Scriptural doctrine.'[37]

Having secured the clergyman's patronage Wigram's next proposed step was for them 'to interest as many of the most respectable inhabitants as possible'. These 'friends of the proposed school' should then visit 'all those poor families over whom, from vicinity of residence or employment or any other cause they have the most influence, to inform them of the plan and urge them to avail themselves of it for the welfare of their children'.[38] During such visits Wigram urged them to take care to avoid appearing to be canvassing for pupils. In all his suggested hints and proposals Wigram was decidedly practical. In some places, if money was forthcoming, a new school room could be built. In other poorer locations a room could be rented in a Grammar school or borrowed from a local National day school. A small stock of books, tracts and other literature should be built up with these and other resources purchased from the SPCK. The ever practical Wigram advice was 'don't attempt too much too soon'.[39]

Wigram has much to say about the character and role of the Sunday school Superintendent. He or she 'must have a heart under the influence of those Christian principles with which they inculcate on others'.[40] Among other tasks they will receive the new scholars, examine them and inquire if they have been baptised and whether there are family prayers in their home. Once these preliminaries have been completed the superintendent will place the children and young people into classes, appoint teachers, keep a general register and Roll Book and maintain order and regularity. The teachers chosen will generally be adults but might in some cases be an older child who could serve as an apprentice or pupil teacher. In the case of adult teachers Wigram was adamant that 'great regard should be paid to their moral and religious character'.[41] In order to secure a flow of teachers Wigram proposed the formation of a teachers' class consisting of the best and most intelligent scholars.[42] The Superintendent was to be responsible for organising the school curriculum, but, Wigram suggested, not too much time should be spent on learning to write. He also provided examples of teaching schemes with lists of topics, and he commended the SPCK, which provided good Sunday school materials for use with different attainable levels.

Wigram's volume is helpful in its detailed coverage. He gives information about keeping a register and provides sample pages, which include columns for morning and afternoon sessions for each day, which are linked with children's attendance cards to be taken home to parents. He even suggested blank pages be included behind each term's schedule for useful notes such as 'J. Page disorderly' or 'Marsh absent on 7th January'.[43] Other important matters are also discussed, most notably rules, discipline and clothing and sickness funds. Wigram is mindful of the fact that children are not legally required to attend Sunday or evening school and therefore a school should have rules so simple, and so clearly expressed, that everyone can understand them.[44] As regards discipline Wigram is adamant that corporal punishment 'can never be adopted with good effect in a Sunday school'.[45] If children are habitually disruptive their parents should be contacted and asked to help in correcting dysfunctional behaviour. In extreme cases children may be turned out of the school. Working among deprived families in his London parish Wigram was fully aware of the desperate poverty in which many children lived. In his concluding pages he therefore made the suggestion that schools should consider the possibility of forming a clothing fund and Sick Society. Just 3d. a week throughout the year, would buy a cloth jacket and waistcoat, corduroy trousers lined and a cloth cap. Equally a small weekly sum would provide children with an allowance per week during illness.[46]

Wigram's book is testimony to his skills as a leader and organiser. In it he was addressing what was simultaneously a vital educational, social and spiritual need. Such was a crucial and needful aspect of Christian mission. Not only were the pupils being given very necessary skills of reading and writing they were receiving moral and spiritual values and some would undoubtedly find a personal Christian faith. In this endeavour Wigram demonstrated an ability to present a vision in a way that others in many differing situations were able to action with adjustments and adaptions.

Alongside his many commitments Wigram began to face more demanding assignments, one of which came about in 1834. Up until that time the National Society had not shown much enthusiasm for the Evangelical initiatives in infant education.[47] However, in 1834 it suddenly declared that it had 'long felt the need for schools for young and older children'.[48] This change of course was doubtless generated by a government grant of £10,000, which would enable the Society to 'enlarge the sphere of its operations'. This abrupt change in outlook was quite probably sparked by Bishop John Bird Sumner, who chaired the Society's General Committee meeting on 23 April 1834.[49] Sumner had already achieved much support for his visionary work in building schools and churches in his Chester diocese. Indeed, Sumner always favoured building a school first as this could also be used for Sunday worship until sufficient funds had been raised for a church. The meeting resolved 'that an application be made to the treasury for a free cover [postage] in order to address the clergy of all places with a population of above 1,500 souls on the subject of establishing schools where they may be required'.[50] It was further agreed 'that if such cover was granted a circular should be drawn up comprising of the principal information respecting the Parliamentary grant'. Wigram was required to set these matters in hand.[51]

The significance and influence of Wigram's role in national education is seen in the fact that he twice appeared before the House of Commons Select Committees on Education in 1834[52] and 1838.[53] On both occasions he was questioned by members of the Committees at considerable length. During the meeting chaired by the Right Hon. Lord John Russell, Wigram found himself being pushed into a corner when both his personal views and those of the National Society were strongly scrutinised. He was asked why there was no general official inspection system of their 3,500 schools?[54] He did, however, agree that such a system could and should be set in place. He was then challenged about the level of training being provided at the National Society's Central

St James's, Westminster, and the National Society

Training School in Westminster. Was five months really a sufficient time to teach school management and impart sufficient knowledge to teach children up to the age of eleven? Wigram was able to state that those in training were instructed seven to eight hours a day and their competency was measure by a final examination.[55]

The Committee of the House of Commons' major concern, however, was the rigid adherence to Church of England doctrine and Liturgy in all the National Society's schools. This was a conviction to which Wigram was also totally committed. He affirmed in response to a question from Lord Russell 'that a complete religious education must have three things; the sacraments of the Church, the doctrines of the Church and the practical precepts of Christianity'.[56] Wigram went on to assert that 'it is not possible with educational integrity to teach precepts without the doctrine which underlines them'.[57] When it was put to him that the Borough Road Teaching School was teaching religion but without impressing particular doctrines on the children, Wigram answered that such schools were 'defective as religious institutions'.[58] On the face of it Wigram's views appear divisive, being at odds with the approach and policies of other less rigid denominations. Yet in the long run it has to be said that Church of England Primary Schools stood firm and kept their ethos and principles.

Four years later when Wigram was once again called to give evidence to the Select Committee on Education his stance and that of the National Society appeared unchanged. It was noted by way of introduction that Wigram 'had taken a considerable interest in the question of the education of the humbler classes'.[59] It was also brought to the Committee's attention that more than half of all children in education were in National Schools.[60] Wigram stated that National schools ideally consisted of 100 to 150 pupils and that their buildings were vested in trustees who were normally the local promoters.[61] Wigram was asked if he felt 'that a great deal of the crime and evil which we see daily about us particularly among the juvenile population in our towns, proceeds from a want of good education, combining useful and moral and religious education'? His answer was that 'the school education alluded to would do something, but the education at home, the moral influence of parents will do more'.[62] In fact he was adamant that 'you can never look to any great and extensive cure of these evils unless you exercise proper influence over adults at the same time as the children'.[63] On another front Wigram assured the Committee that 'all children are treated in exactly the same way in National schools regardless of whether their parents are members of the Church of England or not'.[64] Wigram appeared to have mellowed somewhat since his giving evidence in 1834 as he now asserted 'that the great number of Independents in point of doctrine, differ very little from the Church of England'.[65] Wigram also appeared much more open to a system of inspection of all National schools but believed that societies such as his should appoint their own inspectors. He also stated that those training at the National Society's School in Westminster now studied for two years rather than five months as was formerly the case.[66] One thing that had not changed, however, was Wigram's assertion that education must be based on a Christian foundation. 'My view of education which is to be beneficial to the country is that it must be necessarily religious in character, and of course I mean by that, religious in the sense of a Christian.'[67]

In July 1835 Wigram reported the substance of some recent discussions which he had held with the Chancellor of the Exchequer on the subject of how the Society might administer the government grant of £10,000 to model and training establishments throughout the kingdom. The meeting went on to resolve that Wigram as secretary 'do endeavour to bring under consideration a full and complete account of the arrangements which have already been made by the National Society for the training and instruction of both male and female teachers of schools, as explained in the present annual report'.[68]

The period in which Wigram served as secretary to the National Society was a particularly demanding one. It was an age in which the state was gradually seeking to loosen the church's traditional hold over education. In this Parliament received a certain amount of support from dissenters, who not only resented the dominance of the established church but also the requirement that their children were taught Church of England doctrines in the parish schools, which they could not accept. By 1838 it was clear that matters were reaching a head and that the government was set on a course of active interference, which particularly focused on the training of teachers. Instead of teachers being trained on the job by fulfilling the role of assistants it was now proposed that they should be taught in a new college in London.

The policy of the National Society was to resist at all costs secular government usurping what had been its longstanding and dominant control over education. In an effort to halt the government from reducing the Society's influence, a group of High Churchmen, including S. F. Wood, Henry Manning and William Gladstone, asked for and obtained a joint conference with the National Society's Committee. Their plan, which Wood outlined, was to set up diocesan seminaries, which would be closely connected with the cathedral and its officials, who would provide an academic education for ordinary teachers. There was also to be a central college, if possible a branch of King's College, London, where the most able could be trained for higher educational situations.[69]

This new committee came to be called The Committee of Inquiry and Correspondence and it soon set to work on a whole series of issues relating to Church Education. These included ensuring that there were Boards of Education in every diocese, revising the permitted book lists and ensuring there was adequate inspection of schools. To these proposals the National Society gave only a cautious welcome. Early in 1839 a major meeting was held in London, with Lord Ashley in the chair, at which Francis Close, the forthright incumbent of Cheltenham, pleaded that clergy everywhere should form themselves into local boards and keep in touch with the National Society.[70] The Society was also able to stave off state intervention in church schools by establishing its own system of inspection and by May 1839 it had been able to complete 425 inspections.

Throughout these years Wigram must have got through an enormous amount of work. Not only was he at the heart of these educational challenges and changes with high level meetings and discussions, he also undertook a huge volume of writing. In addition to other correspondence, his 'Letter Book' shows that from January to December 1830 he received 400 letters about schools, in 1836 164, in 1837 90, and in 1838 149.[71] It was therefore perhaps no surprise that in the early part of May 1839 he tendered his resignation. The minutes of the General Committee for 8 May noted, 'A letter was read from the Revd J. C.

Joseph Cotton Wigram

Wigram tendering his resignation of the office of Secretary'.[72] There can be no doubt that Wigram, like so many Evangelicals of the nineteenth century, had been working to the limits of his emotional and physical ability and needed a well-earned rest. In addition he had married in March 1837 and their first child was born a year later.

Wigram was clearly much respected by the committee members of the Society, who expressed themselves as 'unwilling at once to accept Mr Wigram's resignation from the office of secretary which he has fulfilled for so many years, to the entire satisfaction of the Committee, and with great advantage to the great cause which the National Society has in hand'.[73] In view of 'the present state of the questions relating to education' the Committee thought it important to persuade Wigram to remain in office for a time with the aid an assistant secretary'.[74] His endeavours were clearly very highly valued since the sub-committee appointed to meet with him consisted of the Bishops of London, Lincoln and Bangor, Lord Kenyon and three other laymen.[75] Their endeavours appear, however, to have been unsuccessful: no further mention of his name occurs in the minutes of the General Committee and shortly after this meeting the Revd J. Sinclair appears as secretary. The Annual Report at the end of the year carried the following tribute.

> There are two or three remaining subjects to which the Committee cannot but advert before concluding this report. One is the resignation of their late secretary the Rev. J. C. Wigram, MA, who for so many years with unwearied zeal and great ability, gratuitously carried on the business of the Society. In him the society has lost an officer to whom they owe a debt of gratitude not easily repaid.[76]

Wigram hadn't simply confined his attentions to the politics of the National Society he also concerned himself with the content of what was being taught in church schools with a particular focus on Christian instruction. In this connection he had produced the two important books which have been considered in this chapter.

In order to keep its supporters and major donors in the loop, the National Society published in 1839 a small volume entitled *Correspondence of the National Society with the Lords of the Treasury and with the Committee of Council on Education.*[77] It was edited by the Revd John Sinclair, Wigram's successor as secretary to the Society. The exchange

St James's, Westminster, and the National Society

of letters recorded in this volume is significant because a substantial number of those from the National Society were written by Wigram himself, and they demonstrate his skill in crafting, writing and presenting the case for Christian basis for education to a government which was becoming increasingly secular in its thinking and strategy. The preface sets out the aim of the book with clarity:

> In consequence of recent occurrences, connected with national education throughout England and Wales, it has become necessary to furnish the friends of the church with, and of religious instruction, with a full statement of the prolonged negotiations which have been carrying on, for years past, between the Government of this country and the National Society.[78]

The chief subjects which correspondence covered was the proposed government grant to the National Society for a Training Institution for teachers; the provision of a site in Baldwin Gardens, Westminster, near the Society's Central School and Offices; the needs of Sunday schools and the appointment of inspectors of National Schools. All of these issues remained life-long concerns throughout the rest of Wigram's ministry. The letters which he wrote on these topics were addressed to the Chancellor of the Exchequer and the Lords Commissioners of Her Majesty's Treasury.

In Letter XIII, written by Wigram on 13 February 1839, he skilfully, and with full details, submitted the National Society's proposal and application for a grant for the erection of a Model School and a Training School alongside, in the immediate vicinity of their existing Central School in the Sanctuary, Westminster. He carefully explained that the Society wanted a Training School in close proximity to the Model School since 'they have found by experience, that a practising school must always form and indispensable appendage to such an establishment'.[79] Not having received a reply on the matter, Wigram wrote again on 2 March, 'I am further desired to solicit your attention, in the most earnest manner to the application of the National Society, for aid in forming a large Training Institution'.[80] He also pointed out that the National Society was apprehensive that if the delay continued 'the most favourable season for soliciting contributions from gentlemen while in London will pass away and the operations be retarded for another year'.⁸¹ He then received a clearly evasive reply stating it was a pity that that the National Society insisted on teaching Church of England doctrine in their schools, which was offensive to dissenters.⁸² Wigram, however, was not to be side-tracked and wrote again on 6 April restating the National Society's concern 'that the most favourable season for soliciting contributions will be lost'.⁸³ He then received a further reply, this time from Dr J. P. Kay, the Secretary of the Committee of the Privy Council, stating that no decision could be taken 'until a Parliamentary vote has been obtained'.⁸⁴ The very last letter Wigram wrote before his retirement was dated 24 April 1839 and it showed he was still on the case. 'The Committee [of the National Society] however, observe with regret, that your letter does not refer to a very important part of their representation on the subject, and they solicit your attention to that part of the application which relates to the site for the Training Institution.' The Lords Commissioners did eventually make the grant which Wigram had so earnestly and persistently sought although it came with a requirement that all National Society Schools and Institutions receiving government money would be required to accept government inspections. In all, the book printed fourteen of Wigram's letters to the Treasury.⁸⁵ In them he demonstrated a unique ability to set forward and defend the church's role in education to a government which was set on introducing more liberal and secularising values. Wigram should therefore be seen as a significant educationalist and an astute policy maker in what was certainly one of the most significant periods of National Society's history. In his *History of the Evangelical Party in the Church of England*, G. R. Balleine comments that 'Wigram as Secretary of the National Society had done a great work for elementary education'.⁸⁶

Concern for education and school remained Wigram's concern throughout the rest of his life and ministry. During his time as Bishop of Rochester Wigram made only one major speech in the House of Lords and significantly it concerned the National Society. Wigram expressed concern at the way in which the Privy Council's Education Committee had refused to give a grant of money for the building of a proposed new National School at Chrishall in Essex on the ground that about half the residents were dissenters. He pointed out that in this particular case the dissenters 'joined the church people and requested that the difficulty might be waived'. Notwithstanding this, the Privy Council on Education took the view that 'although the existing Nonconformist parishioners might be happy future non-conformists might not feel the same way'. Wigram went on to assert that the Education Committee's response 'seemed to suggest that there was something of a proselytising character in the National Society'. Such a criticism, he pointed out, 'was not correct' and could equally be made concerning British and Foreign Society Schools which were committed to Nonconformist principles and teaching. Wigram was clear that 'the discretionary powers which school managers had to investigate cases of proselytising or abuse should be sufficient to safeguard the consciences of dissenting parents'. His point was that if this issue was not redressed 'it would affect the whole of the Church of England schools'. The motion put by Wigram received support from subsequent speakers including the Bishops of Lincoln and Llandaff and Lord Redesdale. The Bishop of Llandaff further added that 'if the practice complained of by his right reverend friend became general they would have no schools in our small rural parishes'.[87]

Despite the endeavours of the Bishops of London and Bangor and other committee members to persuade Wigram to retain the office of Secretary to the National Society, he was evidently not persuaded. Shortly afterwards he left both the parish of St James, Westminster, and the National Society and commenced a new phase in his life and ministry as rector of the Hampshire parish of East Tisted, to which he had been appointed on 28 March 1839.

Notes

[1] The Revd J. G. Ward was appointed Dean of Lincoln on 7 October 1845. See James Elmes, *A Topographical Dictionary of London and its Environs* (1831) p. 248. See also *The Gentleman's Magazine*, vol. 178 (June–December 1845), p. 519.

[2] 'History and Description of St Luke's Berwick Street' (undated), in CWAC, MS F 942.1375, p. 3.

[3] *Churchwardens Account Book*, 1827 CWAC, 494/191, see Church rates.

[4] Ibid., see Church rates.

[5] Ibid., see North Gallery pew income.

[6] J. C. Wigram, *On Humility*, 1827, title page.

Joseph Cotton Wigram

7   J. C. Wigram, *Ministerial Watchfulness*, 1845, p. 26. Bodleian Library, Oxford, MS 45.1611 (34).
8   *Ibid.*, p. 27.
9   *St James Piccadilly Baptismal Register*, 1828–35, CWAC.
10 *St James Piccadilly Marriage Register* (Westminster), vol. 40, 1830 microfilm, CWAC.
11 See entries in *St James; Baptismal Register*, 1828, vol. 12, CWAC.
12 J. C. Wigram, *On Humility*, 1827. p. 18.
13 St James, Piccadilly, Vestry Minutes, 21 November 1833, CWAC, MS D1772.
14 Rack 1973, p. 363.
15 J. C Wigram, *Ministerial Watchfulness*, 1845, pp. 28–9.
16 'History and Description of St Luke's Berwick Street', CWAC, MS F 942.1375, p. 1.
17 J. C. Wigram, *Ministerial Watchfulness*, 1845, p. 30.
18 St James, Piccadilly, Parish Records and Church Wardens Accounts, 1827, CAWC, 494/191.
19 *Ibid.*
20 *Seventeenth Report of the National Society*, 1828.
21 *Eighteenth Report of the National Society*, 1829.
22 NSA, General Committee Minutes of the National Society, 13 June 1827.
23 See 'History and Description of St Luke's Berwick Street', CWAC, MS F 942.1375, p. 1.
24 For details of the marriage see *The Derby and Chesterfield Reporter*, 9 March 1837 and *The Derby Mercury*, 8 March 1837.
25 Filton 1989, p. 271.
26 A. Wigram, *Register of the Wigram Family*, 1913
27 NSA, General Committee Minutes of the National Society, 13 June 1827.
28 *Ibid.*, 1 December 1830.
29 *Ibid.*, 13 April 1830.
30 J. C. Wigram, *Elementary Arithmetic*, 1832: *The Morning Chronicle*, 2 July 1839.
31 J. C. Wigram, *The Geography of the Holy Land*, 1832.
32 *Ibid.*, p. 4.
33 *Ibid.*, p. 118.
34 *Ibid.*, p. 158.
35 See J. W. Wigram, *Practical Hints*, 1833.
36 *Ibid.*, p. 8.
37 *Ibid.*, p. 10.
38 *Ibid.*, p. 11.
39 *Ibid.*, p. 14.
40 *Ibid.*, p. 20.
41 *Ibid.*, p. 22.

42 Ibid.
43 Ibid., p. 29.
44 Ibid., p. 38.
45 Ibid., p. 61.
46 Ibid., pp. 81–4.
47 Burgess 1958, p. 66.
48 Ibid.
49 NSA, Minutes of the General Committee of the National Society, 1 July 1835.
50 Ibid.
51 Ibid.
52 *Reports and Papers of the House of Commons*, vol. 1, 'Education, Report from the Select Committee on the State of Education with the Minutes of Evidence and Index', 1834.
53 *Report from the Select Committee on Education of the Poorer Classes in England and Wales; Together with the Minutes of Evidence and Index*, vol. 7, 1838.
54 *Report and Papers*, 1834, sections 673–6.
55 Ibid., section 679.
56 Ibid., 776.
57 Ibid., 771.
58 Ibid., 730.
59 *Report from the Select Committee on Education of the Poorer Classes in England and Wales; Together with the Minutes of Evidence and Index*, vol. 7, 1838.
60 Ibid., section 608.
61 Ibid., 661 and 626.
62 Ibid., 680.
63 Ibid., 681.
64 Ibid., 687.
65 Ibid., 697.
66 Ibid., 880.
67 Ibid., 886.
68 NSA, Minutes of the General Committee of the National Society, 1 July 1835.
69 Burgess 1958, p. 68.
70 *The Twenty-Eighth Report of the National Society*, 1839, p. 2.
71 NSA, Letter Book of the National Society, 1830–9.
72 NSA, Minutes of the General Committee of the National Society, 8 May 1839.
73 Ibid.
74 Ibid.
75 Ibid.
76 *The Twenty-Ninth Report of the National Society*, 1840, p. 15.
77 See Sinclair (ed.) 1839.
78 Ibid., Preface.

79   J. C. Wigram, letter to the Commissioners of Her Majesty's Treasury, 13 February 1839, in Sinclair (ed.) 1839, p. 10.
80   J. C. Wigram, letter to the Commissioners of Her Majesty's Treasury, 2 March 1839, in Sinclair (ed.) 1839, p. 12.
81   *Ibid.*
82   *Ibid.*, 13 February 1839, in Sinclair (ed.) 1839, p. 10.
83   *Ibid.*, 1 April 1839, in Sinclair (ed.) 1839, p. 13.
84   J. P. Kay, letter from the Commissioners of Her Majesty's Treasury to J. C. Wigram, 15 April 1839, in Sinclair (ed.) 1839, p. 15.
85   J. C. Wigram, letters to the Commissioners of Her Majesty's Treasury, nos 2, 3, 6, 7, 10, 12, 13, 14, 17, 19, 20, 23, 26 and 27, in Sinclair (ed.) 1839, pp. 1–39.
86   Balleine 1933, p. 267.
87   *Hansard*, Third Series, CLXVII, pp. 400–7.

3

East Tisted Rectory and Archdeacon of Winchester

Having spent twelve arduous years toiling in the parish of St James Westminster and working for the National Society, Wigram now found himself installed in a quiet rural Hampshire rectory. The parish was just a few miles from Rotherfield and four and a half miles from the town of Alton. The acreage was 2,602 and the population, in 1851, just 229. The village had a national school and listed among its residents two gentry and eight traders.[1] The Scott family whose residence stood in an extensive park at nearby Rotherfield was a prominent influence in both the church and the locality. The family had long held the advowson of the living and took responsibility for the southern chancel aisle of the church.[2] At the time of Wigram's appointment the patron of the living was James W. Scott.[3]

Wigram must have found it strange having suddenly exchanged the rush and bustle of the teeming metropolis for the quiet of a rural parish with only a handful of craftsmen and farm labourers now forming the bulk of his Sunday congregations. But being a devoted evangelical clergyman, he knew and believed he was just as answerable to God as before. 'It is', he wrote, 'a sin to be idle in the Lord's vineyard, knowing that we have deliberately promised to labour therein all our days.'[4] He therefore set about his new rural ministry with the same wholehearted commitment that he had demonstrated before. He approached the new task with humility speaking of his desire 'to heal the sick, bind up the broken-hearted, reclaim the transgressors and help forward those who are willing to learn ... upon the little hills and valleys around my own home'.[5] In these 'desires and just works' Wigram was greatly inspired by the writings of George Bull (1634–1710), Bishop of Llandaff, whose writings he declared 'cannot be read without great improvement'. Bull had demonstrated truly zealous devotion and care as a parish minister before going on to take such excellent care of his diocese and particular care over those seeking ordination.[6]

Like Bull before him Wigram recognised that the quiet of a small country living gave incumbents the opportunity to read, reflect and study. He fully recognised 'that holy men have made more converts to Christianity than learned men', but nevertheless he recognised the importance of 'a sufficiency of learning'. He also derived obvious profit from the writings of George Herbert.[7] Along with both Herbert and Bull, Wigram was adamant that all true knowledge 'is drawn from the Book of Books', that is 'the storehouse and magazine of life and comfort'.[8] That said, as will be seen in the pages that follow, Wigram wrote on both educational and theological issues during his time at East Tisted.

Wigram was acutely aware that his first concern must be to demonstrate and live out the life of Christ in practical and obvious ways. 'The main thing', he later wrote 'is to prove experimentally that we have the living power, as well as the approved form of godliness. Our whole conversation must manifest our deep abiding sense of "the truth as it is in Jesus"'.[9]

Wigram was acutely aware that in a small rural parish such as East Tisted, developing friendships and relationships was of supreme importance. He fully recognised that clergy had 'a high station in society' but that it was vital 'to forego our wisdom' and follow the example of Jesus, who 'eschewed the companionship of the holy and just', a reference to the Scribes and Pharisees, who were the good and the great at the time of his earthly ministry. Instead he urged that 'we are to follow the example which was given us by the Physician of Souls who ... was "a friend of publicans and sinners", tended the sick and diseased, laboured to seek and to save the lost and washed the feet of those who were not worthy to unloose his shoes'.[10] Addressing fellow clergy in the Winchester diocese in 1845 Wigram emphasised the importance of what he described as 'colloquial intercourse'.[11] He gave a number of examples of individuals who were 'good conversationalists'. Among them was the Protestant Reformer, John Bradford (1510–55). 'It is told', he said, 'that he never suffered profane or immoral discourse to pass without censure, but withal he exhibited such sweetness of temper, so much tenderness of feeling towards those he rebuked, and such simple desire to maintain the cause of truth and holiness in a spirit of meekness and love, that he always succeeded in restraining what he did not approve.'[12]

Alongside his care and concern for the souls of his parishioners Wigram was also a man who set high store on reading and learning. East Tisted gave him the time to reflect on the needs of those around him and the most effective means of reaching them with the Gospel. Like the majority of his fellow clergy he endorsed a fixed social hierarchy 'between those who have sufficiency and the poor, whom he has decreed shall never cease out of the land'.[13] The central pin in Wigram's policy towards the poor and marginalised, shared by the vast majority of Victorian clergy, was charity. In present-day thinking this has the appearance of dressing an open wound without taking the time to discover what was causing it and so getting to the root of the problem. Wigram, however, regarded it as the only strategy and wrote that this remedy is 'the only effectual method for permanently improving the spiritual and temporal condition of multitudes of poor, and, indeed, of the whole people for who we are concerned'.[14] This means of alleviating the needs of the poor, however, was increasingly one which the Victorian socially minded were beginning to recognise as creating a system of dependency. It was a change in attitude which godly individuals such a Wigram, who held to a strong belief in a fixed social hierarchy, found it hard to face up to.

Wigram soon recognised that 'the difference between London and country working people ... is really much less than is supposed'.[15] Indeed, he found that some of the other practices he had adopted at Westminster worked well among the inhabitants of East Tisted. He continued his London practice of insisting that those he baptised had sponsors who 'frequented the Lord's table'. He wrote, 'I have not knowingly deviated from this rule, except it be by admitting a parent, who was a communicant, to stand proxy for a relative at a distance'.[16] Wigram's practice was to hold baptisms on Sunday afternoons since this was the best time for gathering friends and relatives. His practice was always

Joseph Cotton Wigram

to give a talk whenever a baptism took place. It is clear from the parish registers that Wigram took particular care in the matter of baptisms. There were sixty-seven baptisms during his time as incumbent and he officiated at all of them.[17] He was without doubt a model and conscientious pastor who was diligent in his attention to the occasional offices.[18] Nine marriages took place during his residence and he officiated at all of them:[19] and of the forty-three burials he officiated at thirty-six.[20]

The National School was clearly a high priority on Wigram's agenda. He believed schools to be 'of the greatest use in parochial work. Not only were they able to provide a basic education they were the most hopeful means of reviving a spirit of discipline among our people'.[21]

The vestry minutes show that Wigram paid careful attention to the details of parish and community life. He chaired every single vestry meeting during the period of his incumbency and demonstrated a strong concern for the state of the church building and the social and political issues of life in his parish. Among the matters which seem to have been frequent concerns of the vestry were the appointment of churchwardens and village constables, fixing the annual church rate, the duties and payments of the church clerk and sexton, and the insurance and maintenance of the church building. Wigram's care and attention to detail is reflected in the minutes of the meetings and is particularly visible with regards to the sexton-clerk. In larger parishes these were two separate offices but in small rural parishes such as East Tisted they were conflated. Following the meeting on 25 March 1840 'the clerk was seen and told that the church and churchyard must be kept in better order'.[22] Six years later the vestry found it necessary to clarify the duties of the clerk-sexton.

> 1. To attend at all church services, Sundays, weekdays, festivals, & to put out the books, communion cloths, & put them afterwards away, do all the ordinary clerk's work, & ring the bells for services. 2. Wash the surplice at least 8 times a year, wash the table linen & take care of the same and find bread for Communion. 3. Do all the sexton work;—keep the church yard tidy, cut nettles & weed walks, & do all the clerk's and sexton's work.[23]

The church must have been in a relatively good state of repair since the rate was sixpence in the pound in 1840 but dropped to 2½d. in 1843.[24]

East Tisted Rectory and Archdeacon of Winchester

There were evidently a number of poor within the parish since from time to time the vestry appointed 'overseers of the poor' and collected a poor rate.[25]

For five years at East Tisted Wigram was enabled to live out the life of a model country parson who prayed, visited, practised the spiritual disciplines, worked at his sermons and importantly took time to reflect on his ministry. In 1845 he was able to test out his theories for increasing and improving the church's structures and mission strategies when he was invited by the Bishop of Winchester, Charles Sumner, to give the address to the clergy of the diocese on Friday, 17 October in the parish church of Alton. After summarising the very effective aspects of his parish mission strategy in Westminster and reflecting on five years of ministry in East Tisted, Wigram summarised his presentation by reminding his clerical brethren of their primary ministerial responsibility.

> We minister to souls! Souls! Methinks, in that one word, there is a sermon. Immortal souls! Precious souls! One whereof is more worth than all the world besides, the price of the blood of the son of God... What shall we do?... Let us first prostrate ourselves at God's feet, let us not lie idly there, but arise, and for the future do the work of God with all faithfulness and industry; yea let us make amends for our negligence, by doubling our future diligence.[26]

Wigram's sermon was published later the same year under the title *Ministerial Watchfulness*. Doubtless he received varying responses from his fellow clergy, but one who must surely have been impressed was the Bishop himself. Two years later, the Archdeaconry of Winchester became vacant. Sumner appointed Wigram to the post on 16 November 1847 and installed him on 4 December 1847.[27]

ARCHDEACON OF WINCHESTER

Wigram's elevation should not surprise us. His staunch evangelical convictions were shared by his bishop. Wigram's able ministry in Westminster and skill and dedication as secretary to the National Society were well known to the Bishop of Chester, John Bird Sumner, Bishop

Sumner's older brother. Wigram had already proved himself in combining the roles of parish priest and administrator of the National Society. Now as the incumbent of a small rural living he had the opportunity to prove himself in the role of parish priest and Archdeacon.

Wigram was soon able to demonstrate both his administrative skills and his knowledge of ecclesiastical buildings. He clearly had a strong sense of the importance of a church's history and of preserving the past heritage for future generations. Indeed this was seen in his membership of the Oxford Ecclesiastical Society.* Examples from his surviving letters bespeak warmth, efficiency and a desire to help and encourage churchwardens in their duty to maintain their buildings and fabric in good order. The day following his visit to the Revd E. Woodcock at St Lawrence's Church in Winchester, Wigram wrote from Brighton a carefully worded letter, in which he confirmed what had been discussed and agreed.

> The removal of the gallery under the circumstances appeared very desirable ... I trust a good ventilation will be effected at the top of the East gable end ... I must however particularly request the attention of the churchwardens—1. to the roof, which I trust the parish will strip and relay entirely ... 2. to the lean to against the East end of the church ... It can only be by some great oversight that what I saw has been allowed—that iron clamps are actually let into the church to hold up the neighbouring chimney of a dwelling house ... I shall be interested to learn of your early progress considering the month at which we have arrived.[28]

We catch another glimpse of Wigram's quiet and firm efficiency in a letter that he wrote to the churchwardens of Barton Stacey in February 1849.

> Gentlemen,
> I propose to be at Barton Stacey on Tuesday the 6th of March, & to visit your church & see the improvements which have been made, about ½ past one o'clock. You will oblige me by attending, & I will thank you to have the parish rate book for my assistance in case there is any question made about the pews, such as I was told Mr Perris or Miss Hollest had made.[29]

---

* He is listed as a subscriber in the appendix to the Society's *Archaeological Journal*, vol. 2, 1846.

East Tisted Rectory and Archdeacon of Winchester

Wigram, who of was of a warm and outgoing in nature, went on to state that the purpose of his visit was solely 'to see what is right is done, & as far as possible to strengthen your hands in the discharge of your duties'.[30]

An important aspect of an archidiaconal role was the holding of Visitations of the diocesan clergy. *The Hampshire Advertiser* carried a full report of Wigram's Visitation of the church wardens and clergy of the diocese at St Thomas's Church in Portsmouth on 16 April 1850. Referring to the address as 'a very valuable charge', the paper observed Wigram's foresight in having earlier circulated some of the issues which he was going to address.[31] The article then highlighted the issues which he had brought to their attention. These were fees paid to the clergy, Benefit Societies, the state of parochial church schools and education, charity sermons and the importance of seeking out candidates for confirmation.

Wigram underlined the important fact that 'six-sevenths of the population in the County of Hampshire' were connected with Benefit Societies and that whole families were dependent on them in times of sickness or bereavement. He therefore fully recognised the value of clergy preaching 'charity sermons' but emphasised the need to avoid being led away by those institutions which lacked 'proper objects'. While on this issue he also urged the importance of giving to the church which also supported those in need. Wigram also devoted time to considering the ways in which the education of children could be improved. This, as has already been observed, was a matter close to his heart. He spoke 'at some length' on the efforts that were currently being made to improve the means for training masters of parochial schools and placing them in a proper position. He particularly regretted 'the great lack of candidates for this kind of training'. Wigram also referred to the fact that there were a thousand Sunday school teachers in the diocese who provided an 'important auxiliary to the church which could be improved'. This then led to his stressing the importance of 'public catechetical examination in the different parishes and seeking out candidates for confirmation'. While still on the subject of education he spoke of 'the value of establishing and improving libraries as a means of counteracting the cheap literature which was so unhappily diffused and the tendency of which was to debase rather than elevate'.[32]

Joseph Cotton Wigram

Some of the content of Wigram's address was drawn from his extensive researches into the social and religious conditions of Portsea, which he had begun in earnest in 1848. It was eventually published in February 1851 under the title *A Letter on the Spiritual Necessities of Portsea Within and Without the Walls addressed to the Principal Inhabitants of the Town and Vicinity*.[33] On becoming archdeacon it was immediately clear to Wigram, along with many others, that Portsea, the area between old Portmouth and the dockyard to the north, was the most needy, socially and spiritually deprived area within the diocese of Winchester. Eighteenth-century walls and ramparts hemmed in the town on the east and separated it from the remainder of the parish and the old parish church (St Mary's), which layout outside the walls. Wigram's researches were thorough and detailed. He visited all the churches in Portsea separately, questioned their clergy and wardens, and made himself fully acquainted with their congregations. Then in October 1849 he examined each of the schools one by one. These investigations he supplemented with other occasional visits to the area. 'I have surveyed the localities and have corresponded extensively with the clergy', he wrote, and concluded 'that the religious destitution of Portsea, within and without the walls, is most deplorable.'[34]

Wigram began his strategy citing *The Report to the Board of Health*, which spoke of 'the fearful conditions of the place and the extensively fatal consequences'. It then gave a most graphic account of the social condition in which the inhabitants were required to exist.

> The dwellings of the labouring population are defective in construction; many houses back to back, and the ground and the floors are exceedingly damp; the streets are long and narrow, dilapidated, damp, and filthy beyond description ... Most of the courts are extremely confined, the approaches being low-tunnel passages, averaging from three to six feet wide ... Soldiers' wives and families inhabit some of the most wretched, crowded and unhealthy quarters of the town; and the usual haunts of the sailor, when on shore, are dens so vile and degraded that language cannot describe them.[35]

He continued with a summary of 'the deficiency in the spiritual provision of Portsea'. The population consisted of about 50,000 souls and above 10,895 houses. There were seven churches with not more than ten inadequately remunerated clergy providing 8,700 seats, of which only 3,300 were open to the poor. There were sixteen schools with 2,028 scholars under fourteen years of age.

St Mary's, Portsea's parish church, which stood outside the walls, had been rebuilt in 1844, with public grants and help from its patron, Winchester College. Within the walls there were two proprietary chapels, St George's and St John's, built in 1754 and 1787 respectively. Neither had any designated district for which they were pastorally responsible. Following grants from the Church Commissioners, St Paul's and All Saints were built without the walls, in 1823 and 1828 respectively, and Trinity Church, within the walls, in 1841. Wigram summarised the major weakness of this setup: 'as might be expected, where so great an inadequacy of Church ministrations prevailed, evil, under almost every form, has taken very deep root.'[36] He described the area covered by All Saints as 'the most miserable in Portsea; houses crowded, streets uncompleted, ill drained, with stagnant mud,—children abounding in vicious idleness, numbers unbaptised, neglected.' He went on to write in more general terms of the whole town, its environs and its peoples.

> The want of due pastoral influence and restraint among them is appalling. The ordinary vices connected with garrison and seaport towns grievously prevail ... In particular, the numbers and the licentiousness of the public houses are extreme. A clergyman, who had resided some years in Portsea, states,—'According to my calculation, there are 360 beer shops and 236 public houses, in the island of Portsea: i.e. 596 drinking houses, with accommodation for 24,000 people ... Nor is this the worst; lasciviousness and unchastity are fearful ... Many of the public houses pander for their maintenance by female degradation ... Meanwhile, these over-flowings of ungodliness are increasing, from time to time, by the dispersion of the enormous crews of our line-of-battle ships, excited by the release from long continued restraint ... they go forth, like sheep to the slaughter, the prey of the agents of Satan, carried away captive by every lust.'[37]

Wigram's proposal had 'five great objects'; 1. Four new churches costing £3,000, each with an endowment of £1,000; 2. A sum of £6,000 each in aid of a Parsonage House to the four new churches, and also a Parsonage for Trinity, All Saints, St Paul's and Milton; 3. A schoolroom and residence for each new church, with a fifth at Copner, £400 each; 4. An Act of Parliament to render a parochial system feasible, £500; 5. Compensation by endowment for fees subtracted from the Vicarage £1,800.[38]

Wigram added one more non-essential objective 6: If possible, a small Repair Fund of £250 for each new church. The whole scheme, he noted, could not be effected for less than £26,000, and he proposed that this sum could be raised by grants from public bodies, by subscriptions from Portsea and the vicinity spread over a period of three or four years, by appeal to the gentry of the county and by 'extended application to the wealth and charity of the nation'.[39] Regardless of the magnitude of his scheme, Wigram felt confident that 'the Christian sympathy of the people of England, and especially of those who reside in a County richly studded with the mansions of the wealthy and great, will seldom be appealed to in vain'.[40]

Wigram was very hopeful that his proposal could be met in full. He felt that if fewer than four new churches were built the level of pastoral care would be very far from sufficient. Likewise, there must be a school for each church in order that every child would be able to receive a minimal education. An Act of Parliament would be essential in order for the other churches to have designated areas of pastoral care. Justice also required that the incumbent of the parish church should be compensated for his loss of fees for baptisms, weddings and funerals, many of which would now go to the other churches when an Act of Parliament allowed them to have designated pastoral areas. These payments, Wigram asserted, 'are the incumbent's legal right'.[41]

Only too well aware that there would be opposition to at least some aspects of his proposal, Wigram stated at the outset that each of his six objectives might be taken and adopted 'without regard to the rest of the scheme'.[42] The response of the clergy, churchwardens and others who were involved proved to be altogether more antagonistic than Wigram had anticipated. There were several strong objections to the scheme. It was felt that the proposed new church at Kingston Cross would interfere with the interests of All Saints, and that the church at Southsea was a private venture, which was not designed for the needs of the poor and should not be part of the scheme. It was further objected that the endowments proposed for the four new churches should also be given to the two proprietary chapels of St George and St John. There was also dissent from the proposal to lift the legal restriction which at present prevented them from having designated districts of pastoral care and oversight.

Wigram's strategy, which he published in 1851, was bold and forward-thinking but it was always going to be difficult to action on account of the longstanding extant governmental and ecclesiastical laws. Church building was hampered by the requirement of a separate Act of Parliament to create new ecclesiastical districts. New places of worship erected within a parish could only be maintained by a system of pew rents and this had the effect of turning them into middle-class preaching houses with no place for the poor. Furthermore, they became in effect chapels within an existing parish, the incumbent of the parish church retaining full responsibility for all the occasional offices of baptism, marriage and burial. In Portsmouth, the ancient parish of Portsea had acquired four such chapels between 1758 and 1838 but none was granted a district until 1838. The overall situation, which doubtless angered Wigram, was that the established church serving Portsmouth's 50,000 inhabitants only had between 3,000 and 3,500 free seats available to the poor.[43] This stood in stark contrast to Portsea's 360 beer shops and 236 public houses with accommodation for 24,000 people.[44]

When detailed discussions began J. V. Stewart, the vicar of Portsea, could not be persuaded to surrender his rights to full control of all the occasional offices and the income arising from them. This in spite of Wigram proposing a system of financial compensation for his loss of income and the added attempts of Bishop Sumner to persuade him to do so. In reality his reluctance to allow the existing chapels to take a share in them was inevitable. But there was more at stake. In particular, a conflict over churchmanship among the town's churches was gradually emerging. In the early years of the nineteenth century it was the Evangelicals who revived the life and pastoral care of their parishes, but by the 1840s a number of devoted Anglo-Catholics were beginning to do the same as well as promoting church extension. Despite his fair-minded attempts to support the mission of all the Portsmouth churches

Wigram's sympathies were clearly with the Evangelicals. This became apparent when, following the rejection of his scheme, he secured a grant from the Church Pastoral Aid Society towards maintaining a curate for the neighbourhood of Marylebone and its environs.[45]

This proposal was Wigram's last shot at doing at least something to forward mission in this town of desperate need and within the ancient parish of Portsea. He therefore wrote to the vicar, J. V. Stewart, and to the ministers of the three chapels within his parish—the Revd C. Stewart of St Paul's, the Revd H. Snooke of All Saints, and the Revd J. P. M'Ghie, the incumbent of the proposed new area and to the rural dean.[46]

In his letter dated 12 November 1850, Wigram carefully delineated the proposed new area and pointed out that the fees for the occasional offices would still be paid to the vicar of the parish of Portsea. He also stressed that the Bishop 'cordially approves the plan and is ready to assign a district, with your consent, to the exclusive charge of a curate, to act under his license'.[47] Yet even here Wigram met with even more negative responses. The rural dean suggested building a new church 'through the means of some committee'. The incumbent of All Saints chapel opined, 'why not have two instead of one curate'? and then went on to suggest an approach be made to the High Church Additional Curates' Aid Society. The incumbent of St Paul's stated that he himself had already applied to the Society for the means of maintaining an assistant and re-establishing a third service. Wigram finally concluded that he had only three options: 'to abandon the project altogether; to press on and try to form a new district for the poor of the Marylebone area; or to call upon the people of Portsea, as I intend, to do themselves what you are unable or reluctant to take part in'. He therefore stated that he now proposed to publish a letter next month 'calling on the people to attempt for themselves what I have failed to obtain on their behalf'.[48]

The obstructive attitude of the vicar of Portsea, and the incumbents of the chapels within the parish meant that the Anglican advance in the town was decidedly slow. However, Wigram was doubtless pleased at the subsequent advances made by St John's Church. In 1853 the Revd John Knapp, a strong Evangelical, was appointed as minister in charge and remained in office until 1881.[49] Knapp was deeply concerned with

East Tisted Rectory and Archdeacon of Winchester

the social and spiritual conditions he found in Portsea. The major problem which confronted him was that his church was dependent for financial support from pew rents, which meant that there was little place for the poor at Sunday worship. However, Knapp became involved with the informal worship that was being organised for the London poor by the 7th Earl of Shaftesbury at Exeter Hall, off the Strand. This led him, with the support of the Bishop of Winchester, to purchase a vacant circus building in Landport. There he started services in June 1857. On the very first night the congregation numbered 2,000. The evening proved so popular that morning worship was soon commenced. The nature of the proceedings was described as 'highly experimental' with popular hymns and a rousing sermon.[50] Knapp's view was that Sunday morning services should be held as late as possible as 'the sons of toil have enough of early rising'. 'It is well', he continued, 'if they can find the Sabbath day to be to them, a day of rest, physically for the body, as well as morally and spiritually, for the mind and the soul.' His circus church was so successful that in 1863 he handed over full responsibility for it to his curate, John Martin, who became the first incumbent.

Wigram was undoubtedly disappointed that his three separate attempts to get at least some form of his proposals for Portsea established had been met with such stubborn opposition on the part of the clergy concerned. That said, he must have been encouraged by what he saw of Knapp's ministry and the subsequent establishment of two new Evangelical parishes of St Luke and St Simon in Portsmouth.[51]

For eleven years Wigram had been a model rural incumbent, who faithfully and diligently cared for the souls of those committed to his care. Since 1845, however, he had become widely known across the diocese of Winchester on account of his work as Archdeacon. He travelled extensively checking on the concerns of clergy and churchwardens over the fabric of their buildings. He had also continued to encourage clergy and laity on the great importance of establishing and maintaining schools and particularly those affiliated with the National Society. Clearly Wigram was a man of enormous energy who needed a fresh challenge. That opportunity came opened for him at the close of 1850, when he was offered the Rectory Living of St Mary's, Southampton.

Joseph Cotton Wigram

Notes

1. *The Post Office Directory of Hampshire*, 1855.
2. HRO, East Tisted Vestry Minutes, 26 March 1846.
3. Information from the Bible given to Joseph Cotton 'by his affectionate Mother', now in possession of Canon Sir Clifford Wigram Bt.
4. *Post Office Directory of Hampshire*, 1855, entry for East Tisted.
5. J. C. Wigram, *Ministerial Watchfulness*, 1845, p. 5.
6. Ibid., p. 23.
7. Ibid., p. 22.
8. Ibid.
9. Ibid., pp. 16–17.
10. Ibid.
11. Ibid., p. 34.
12. Ibid.
13. Ibid., p. 25.
14. Ibid.
15. Ibid., p. 26.
16. Ibid., p. 30.
17. HRO, East Tisted Baptismal Register 1839, entries 215–82.
18. J. C. Wigram, *Ministerial Watchfulness*, 1845, p. 31.
19. HRO, East Tisted Marriage Register, 1840–51, nos 5–13.
20. HRO, East Tisted Burial Register, 1839–50, entries 130–72.
21. J. C. Wigram, *Ministerial Watchfulness*, 1845, p. 35.
22. HRO, East Tisted Vestry Minutes, 1834–1927, entry for 20 April 1840.
23. Ibid., 26 March 1846.
24. Ibid., 12 March 1840 and 17 April 1843.
25. Ibid., 29 March 1844 and 5 March 1846.
26. J. C. Wigram, *Ministerial Watchfulness*, 1845, pp. 37–8.
27. Recorded in the Bible given to Wigram 'by his Affectionate Mother'.
28. J. C. Wigram, letter to Revd E. Woodcock, 5 September 1848, HRO, MS 107N81/WPW6.
29. J. C. Wigram, letter to the churchwardens of Barton Stacey, HRO, MS 60M70/PW13.
30. Ibid.
31. *The Hampshire Advertiser*, 20 April 1850.
32. Ibid.
33. See J. C. Wigram, *A Letter on the Spiritual Necessities of Portsea*, 1851.
34. Ibid., pp. 4–5.
35. Ibid., pp. 9–10.

East Tisted Rectory and Archdeacon of Winchester

36 *Ibid.*, p. 12.
37 *Ibid.*, p. 13.
38 *Ibid.*, p. 14.
39 *Ibid.*
40 *Ibid.*, p. 15.
41 *Ibid.*, p. 16, para 6.
42 *Ibid.*, p. 21.
43 Yates 1983, p. 1.
44 *Ibid.*, p. 4.
45 See J. C. Wigram, *A Letter on the Spiritual Necessities of Portsea*, 1851, pp. 27–8 ('Third Proposal').
46 *Ibid.*, pp. 27–8: Letter to the Revd J. V. Stewart *et al.*, 12 November 1850.
47 *Ibid.*, p. 28.
48 *Ibid.*, p. 31.
49 Yates 1983, p. 1.
50 *Ibid.*, p. 9.
51 *Ibid.*

4

Rector of St Mary's, Southampton

Bishop Charles Sumner clearly recognised Wigram as a strategic leader possessed of boundless energy because, in addition to his role as archdeacon, he now appointed him to what was one of the most demanding parishes in his Winchester diocese. This was St Mary's, set amidst the sprawling dockland settlements of Southampton. Christians were known to have worshipped on the site from Saxon times. The first recorded priest was Richerius, who is listed in the Domesday Book as 'clerk'. Over the centuries before Wigram took office the church had been rebuilt at least five times. At the time of his arrival it was reported to be in a tolerable state of repair.[1]

The town of Southampton had begun to boom at the beginning of the nineteenth century with large shipments of timber arriving from the Baltic and coal, slate and stone being brought in from Scotland. Wine and fruit were imported from Portugal and Spain and grain from Ireland. In consequence new quays were added to the docks in the early 1840s. In the 1820s paddle steamers began sailings to and from France and the Channel Islands. By the 1830s 100,000 passengers were travelling from Southampton every year. In 1840 the railway reached the town and coach building, which had been a major industry, began to decline. The same period also saw the introduction of the first horse-drawn bus services. In the 1850s there was a marked growth in the population with new developments in Northam, Freemantle and Newtown.

Notwithstanding these developments Southampton, along with many other large towns and cities, was noted for its unsanitary conditions. Out of 230 streets in the 1840s 145 were without sewers. Unsurprisingly there was a cholera outbreak in 1849 in which 240 people died.

Joseph Cotton Wigram

Another outbreak in 1865 killed a further 152 townspeople. In 1838 the Royal South Hampshire Hospital opened its doors to the public. Such was the environment in which Archdeacon Wigram found himself following his institution on 9 March 1851.[2]

At that time St Mary's parish was listed as having a population of 21,000 souls.[3] It was divided into five separate districts, each of which had an assistant minister. Their income was derived from valuable tithe payments, which came from property in the parish and the rectory of South Stoneham, which was attached to St Mary's. In 1845 the latter were commuted at £1,430. St Mary's proper had a population of 7,440 and was overseen by the rector, an assistant clergyman and a Scripture reader. The Bernard Street district had a population of 5,440 was under the care the Revd John Scotland and a Scripture reader. Trinity District contained 4,160 souls with two clergy and a Scripture reader. The Northam and Newtown Districts were altogether smaller and each had one clergyman and a Scripture reader.[4] Northam was granted status as a separate district in 1851 and a church building erected in 1854. Bernard Street became a new district by Order of Council in 1853 and a church and parsonage house were erected in 1858.[5] Wigram in his joint capacity as rector of St Mary's and Archdeacon clearly played a major part in these initiatives. The earlier difficulties he had encountered in Portsea had doubtless equipped him with negotiating skills to carry these proposals through to a successful conclusion.

The district of St Mary's proper contained National Schools for boys and girls and infants in Grove Street. Encouraged by the effectiveness of his visiting schemes in Westminster, Wigram quickly revived the District Visiting Society. Visitors collected savings for the Bank of Small Deposits and made contact with the sick who had been notified to them by the clergy or Scripture reader. There were also specially trained individuals, who under Wigram's direction went into private schools and visited women in their confinements. Training was also given to adults seeking to become assistant Sunday School teachers. Evening classes were held on Sunday evenings for young men at the Young Men's Library and Reading Room. Families who wanted to rent a garden allotment on the church glebe could make application to a Mr Goodman at 16 Orchard Lane. In addition to these commitments Wigram, or his assistant priest, visited the National Schools in Grove Street every Monday at 11 o'clock and attended to the needs of the Provident Institution at 7.00 o'clock in the evening. Requests for baptisms, churchings and other concerns were dealt with at 11.00 a.m. on Wednesdays and Fridays. Wigram continued his earlier practice of taking particular care over the preparation of confirmation candidates. On Sunday evenings he gave teaching at the rectory for those who wanted to consider the possibility of confirmation. Application had to be made by the parents of the young people concerned.

WIGRAM'S STRATEGY

Wigram knew that his only hope of making a significant impact on the people of St Mary's was by building a pastoral team which included lay workers and by effecting a major reorganisation of the church boundaries. Near the foot of a printed document entitled *Helps for the Pastoral Care of St Mary's, Southampton*, Wigram invited, 'all who may be willing to help him in any of these benevolent works, to communicate at once with himself'. 'The people of St Mary's Proper', he continued, 'are now being visited throughout, and the census returns are being verified, in order to the furtherance of these objects and of Pastoral work generally.'[6] During the early years of his ministry in Westminster Wigram had learned the value of having full-time lay assistants. Such men and women were able to devote their time going from house to house and identify those parishioners in particular need. He was also very committed to the work undertaken by Scripture readers. There were several who worked in the sub-divisions of his parish. They were able combine social visits with an offer to read passages of the Bible. It is clear from reports that many homes were happy to accept such offers. *The Hampshire Advertiser* published an account of a testimonial meeting held in St Mary's School Room in June 1854 for Mr Joseph Wilkinson the 'much respected Scripture Reader of St Mary's Proper'. Wilkinson, who was moving on to another position, had served St Mary's Proper with its population of 8,000 souls from 1 February 1851 to 1 June 1854. During that time he had made more than 12,000 visits and only once had been treated unkindly. Wigram, who chaired the meeting, 'passed a high eulogium on Mr Wilkinson, and presented him with a handsome Family Bible, bearing the inscription:—"Presented to Joseph Wilkinson, by Joseph Cotton Wigram, Rector of St Mary, Southampton, and Archdeacon of Winchester, as a token of esteem for the manner in which he discharged his duties as Scripture Reader...".Wilkinson also received a silver salver and gold pencil case, presented by the parishioners of Mary's. In his response Wilkinson described the previous three years as 'by far the happiest of his life'.[7]

RE-STRUCTURING THE PARISH BOUNDARIES

Having been Archdeacon of Winchester for several years prior to his appointment as rector of St Mary's, Wigram and his visiting team soon became acutely aware of the needs of the rapidly growing population both in the dockland area and the town as a whole. It was already clear to him that the parish boundaries were in most cases set far too large for one man to administer and pastorally care for.

From his experience as rector of the rural living of East Tisted, Wigram could see that the parish system was a workable proposition in the countryside, albeit in a hierarchical, paternalistic way, which was offensive to most dissenters, who objected to church rates and tithe payments. But his previous years in Westminster had also made him all too aware that in an urban context a sprawling over-populated urban parish was too large to care for pastorally or to create any sense of a caring community. It was no surprise therefore that Lord Shaftesbury opined in 1855 that 'the parochial system is, no doubt, a beautiful thing in theory, and is of great value in small rural districts; but in large towns is mere shadow of a name'.[8] Added to this was the fact that many working men and women regarded the parochial system as 'corrupt, inefficient and the machinery for ecclesiastical domination'.[9] As most observers of the time suspected, the Religious Census of 1851 demonstrated that the great mass of the nation's working poor were absent from the churches on Sundays. Wigram may also have been well aware of the parish of Leeds that had numbered 150,000 and which, following legislation in 1843, the incumbent divided up, thereby seriously reducing his own income.[10] Indeed this gesture might well have prompted his own course of action in Southampton.

Ever the strategist Wigram therefore fairly quickly embarked on a course of dividing his own and other large parishes into smaller areas. Where there were chapels-of-ease or proprietary chapels he also set about holding meetings with those concerned aiming to secure agreements from the Ecclesiastical Commissioners 'to create new districts for Spiritual Purposes within Southampton'.[11]

Before Wigram came to St Mary's, as we have seen, the parish was already divided into five areas each with its own church building and supervised by an assistant priest. Nevertheless, the overall responsibility for all the pastoral and administrative work remained in his hands as rector of the entire parish. This meant that all the fees from weddings, funerals and other occasional offices were paid to him. Wigram was clear that this was a pastoral burden which neither he nor any future successor could handle effectively; it needed to be shared. To that end in September 1850 he held extensive meetings and made applications to the Commissioners requesting them to formalise in law the boundaries of these three areas within his parish. These were Newtown, Bernard Street and Northam. His plan included assigning the money accruing from fees to the income of the assistant ministers of these new ecclesiastical districts.

It was proposed that the new district of Newtown should be known as St Luke's Newtown. It would be formed out of the parish of St Mary together with a small portion of the adjoining parish of South Stoneham, of which Wigram was also the incumbent. He noted in his application that 'the better classes of Southampton are settling here' and 'in general the houses are decent'.[12] Two months later Wigram made application for the second district of Bernard Street to be recognised in law, stating that its population was 'increasing rapidly in the area towards the docks where it may be appropriate to build another church'. The inhabitants of this area he characterised as 'small shopkeepers, and lodgings house keepers, with working people'.[13] Wigram also made a third application for a further district to be called 'Christ Church Northam'. The whole of this area lay within the parish of St Mary's. The population, he wrote, which he estimated to be about three thousand and likely to increase 'varies somewhat at different times of the year, according to the work of the ship-yards'. New sites were being taken for erecting new houses and works. Wigram highlighted the fact that 'a store is rented at £10 a year and is used as a place of worship. Being about 45 feet x 12 feet, it houses a congregation of 150–170 people who crowd in for Sunday services which are held under the sanction of the bishop'. A school room was also housed in a rented store. Wigram also made a similar application for the Trinity district, which he estimated had a population of 4,160.[14]

Wigram doubtless found satisfaction when a year later in December 1851 he received a letter informing him 'that the proposal lately submitted by you for the formation of four districts out of the Parishes of St Mary, Southampton and South Stoneham have received the general approval of the Ecclesiastical Commissioners for England and with a view to the carrying the whole arrangement into effect'.[15] This whole legal process proved to be a demanding one. James Chalk, Secretary to the Commissioners, required Wigram to put down clearer and more definite lines demarking the boundaries of the new districts on the map.[16] Then there were also further questions as to how the new districts were to be endowed?[17] St Mary's, as Wigram was doubtless well aware, was in fact a very wealthy parish owning valuable property and substantial land in parts of the town and the dockland areas, which yielded a considerable rent return. In addition it derived further income from the adjoining parish of South Stoneham, which in 1845 was commuted at £1,430.[18] It was from these sources that Wigram proposed to support the newly legalised ecclesiastical areas to the tune of £750 per annum.[19] The whole scheme of these four new districts was finally put into action following a letter received from Whitehall in April 1853.[20]

This was not, however, to be the end of Wigram's downsizing his large parish in order to create smaller more effective pastoral care areas. *The London Gazette* of 15 July 1859 gave details of another scheme by which Wigram agreed in law that 'all the land currently belonging to the parish of St Mary but now situated in the parish of All Saints Southampton shall be translated and become absolutely vested in that benefice'.[21] This arrangement, described as a 'scheme for making better provision for the cure of souls in the parish of All Saints, Southampton', was signed and sealed by John Sumner, Archbishop of Canterbury, Charles Sumner, Bishop of Winchester and Joseph Cotton Wigram as rector of St Mary's.[22]

The Southampton City Archives are replete with letters on these issues in Wigram's own hand and exchanges with and queries from the Ecclesiastical Commissioners. These relate to the estimated population of the new districts, precise locations of the new boundaries to be illustrated on maps, how the salaries of the district ministers are to be paid and the reapportioning of tithes. The establishment of these new districts along with his other archdiaconal responsibilities and the day-to-day pastoral work in his now smaller parish of St Mary was an enormous workload.

Wigram's other correspondence, vestry reports and the St Mary's Church Wardens' Book[23] give glimpses into numerous meetings and concerns, which must have squeezed Wigram's time and energy still further. The very first month following his institution a committee appointed by the vestry reported on the condition of the church building. The roof had been found to be 'in a very dilapidated state' and it was felt that the boarding timbers might well prove to be 'decayed'. The staircase and walls of the belfry were also clearly in bad condition. Because of the difficulties of raising the money from the parish the committee strongly urged that an application should be made to the Hoadly Charity for a substantial grant.[24] The reason for their recommendation was that the last annual vestry meeting had refused the proposed a church rate of 3d. in the pound. A number of those present being nonconformists disapproved of paying money in support of a church which they did not attend and whose doctrines they disapproved of. A Mr T. Fox had taken strong exception to the suggested rate and had proposed 2d. in the pound, which was agreed on a show of hands. This meant that the total required sum of £232 could not be met. *The Hampshire Advertiser* stated, 'We believe Mr Purchase, the former Church warden is £70 out of pocket through the refusal of the required rate during his last year in office'.[25]

Matters did not end there and strong opposition to the church rate persisted at St Mary's, as it did in many parishes across England.

Joseph Cotton Wigram

The vestry met on 17 March 1853 for the purpose of granting a church rate for the year ending Easter 1853. The churchwarden, Mr H. Dusautory, presented an estimate of expenses, amounting to £115, which required a rate of 2d. in the pound. He stated that 'if it was not agreed to the Officers of the Church could not be paid their salaries'. It was then put to him that if the arrears of the last year's rate were collected the proposed rate would be sufficiently covered. On his admission that such was the case it was proposed by Mr Fox and seconded by Mr Bowman 'that this Meeting be adjourned to Easter Tuesday next, to get in the uncollected portion of the rate made in July 1851; it appearing that such uncollected portion exceeds in amount the Churchwardens' estimate'. This resolution was followed by an amendment 'that the Churchwardens' Accounts, as presented by Mr Dusautory be adopted, and that all arrears of rates be excused'. It was carried by the Nonconformists, who demanded that a poll be held on the issue the following Monday and Tuesday, 21 and 22 March. A 'Battle Royal' then ensued. 'Friends of the church' were publicly urged 'not to allow the defaulters of the previous rate off the hook by coming and recording their vote against Mr Fox's Resolution.' The churchwardens would be persuaded 'to do their duty and collect the Arrears'. If this could be done, they further pointed out, 'the required amount would be obtained without the need for a further rate'.[26] Those who opposed the collection of the previous year's arrears published a flier, which was widely circulated and began with the sentence, 'Your services will be required on MONDAY and TUESDAY next, to protect yourselves from the tyranny and rapacity of the Rector of St Mary's'. 'He will', it continued, 'not pay Church Rates himself; but he blames us for following his good example and wishes to force our faithful and honest Churchwarden into legal proceedings against the conscientious defaulter.'[27]

More was to follow. At a meeting later the same month Wigram and the wardens discussed dividing the duties of the sexton and to consider the urgent need for repairs to the church roof.[28] In September the same year Wigram granted a portion of his glebe land on the south side of Chapel Road to the wardens of the parish as a site for a school 'only for use of adults or children of the labouring manufacturing classes'. The

Rector of St Mary's, Southampton

school was 'to be always in union with and conducted upon the principles and in furtherance of the ends and designs of the incorporated National Society for promoting the education of the poor in the principles of the Established Church'.[29] The building was finally completed towards the end of 1854. Wigram received a letter from John Lonsdale, the Secretary of the National Society dated 27 December expressing his pleasure at the completion of the school.[30] In the summer of 1858 meetings of parishioners and others were held to discuss a proposal by the mayor and town council to annex Southampton Common to the parish of St Mary. There were also ongoing discussions between 1852 and 1857 to consider the state of St Mary's churchyard and the need to complete the iron fencing round the churchyard.[31] Wigram's correspondence includes letters from Mr W. Churton concerning the removal of the old railings in 1852[32] and from Mr I. Godden in 1857 stating that 'to finish the new railings in the same pattern will be about 70 feet including a 3 foot gate, the whole to be completed for the sum of sixteen pounds five shillings'.[33]

Notwithstanding this heavy load of parish restructuring, administration and pastoral care, Wigram still managed to attend to many commitments in his role as Archdeacon of Winchester and to take part in other local, diocesan and wider church activities.

ARCHDEACONRY LABOURS

Education and particularly the education of children was never far from Wigram's heart. He saw that the well-being and the future of local churches depended on their being able to embrace and include children and young people. In this he shared the vision of his diocesan bishop, Charles Sumner, who during his episcopate of nearly thirty years had made Sunday and week-day schools a prominent feature of his Charges and other addresses to meetings of the laity and clergy. Following his Visitation of 1854 the Bishop was requested to preside at a public meeting on 30 November in Winchester to adopt measures to carry out the recommendation he had made.[34] On that occasion he was supported by a significant number of persons of influence from all parts of the

Joseph Cotton Wigram

county and included a representative from the National Society. This was followed by a meeting of rural deans and others who had agreed to act as corresponding members of the Sunday School Committee, which had been formed by the Diocesan Board of Education at the Bishop's request.

Wigram seized the moment to carry this impetus forward across his Archdeaconry which, comprising all of Hampshire and the Isle of Wight, totalled 380 parishes or districts with twenty-six rural deans. He brought together a Committee of fourteen clergy, a corresponding secretary and two visiting secretaries, who would accompany and assist him in a series of local conferences, which he organised in local areas across the county. In addition, thirty other clergy were selected to serve as correspondents and to work with rural deans in setting up and explaining the arrangements in each area. Eventually thirty-four centres were adopted as places where meetings could be held.

One of the first steps was 'the opening up of depots for the sale of Sunday school materials' in thirteen small towns in the county. These 'depots', some of which were in shops and stores, held a supply of lesson books, writing materials and publications put out by the National Society. Among them were Mr Walton in High Street, Alton, the SPCK book room in Andover, Mr Cottle's bookshop at Basingstoke and Messrs Jacob and Johnson in Winchester.

Generally speaking, these conferences began at five o'clock in the evening with teachers and others coming from their workplaces to share in a social meal. After prayers and the singing of one or two hymns, an aspect of organising and running a school was presented, usually by a lay man with knowledge of the chosen topic. This was followed by discussion and a resolution to initiate a practical response. Some of the issues raised and considered included, 'How to maintain interest in a class', 'Subject-matter of teaching and preparation', 'The duty of the upper classes to assist in Sunday schools', 'The character of Sunday School teachers', 'Adult classes', 'Infant classes' and 'The importance of the co-operation of parents'. Other concerns which came to the fore included the difficulties of differing abilities, the importance of using simple language and easy illustrations, the difficulties of getting the lads out of the farmyards for any kind of instruction

Rector of St Mary's, Southampton

Wigram ascribed the success that attended the Sunday schools 'in considerable measure to these conferences', which he along with others had been able to organise.[35] As a result, he published these details of what had been taking place in the hopes that other areas of the country might find benefit and encouragement 'from the example which the Winchester diocese has set'.[36] Among his conclusions he maintained that 'every place contains within itself materials for carrying out its own Sunday School work'. Second, he asserted that the best and proper way of forming a Sunday school 'is not to gather children and teach them just as we can, with indifferent teachers'. Rather it is to work with promising adults and inspire them with the love of teaching the young.'[37] Third, all who are qualified to help should be publicly and privately encouraged. Fourth, when interest is showed by people in the congregation this is the moment to put some literature in their hands which will show the kinds of help they could be offering. Fifth, if really efficient help is at hand this may be the opportunity to contemplate forming a week-day National School. Sixth, Wigram was adamant that 'we must have Sunday and evening adult classes as well as Sunday schools'.[38]

Despite these encouragements Wigram still found it necessary in his Archdeaconry Charge of 1855 to bemoan the fact that if 'what I have been reading recently in the returns made to me on Sunday schools, continues, that good result which we all crave after cannot be accomplished'. He went on to urge 'that the best people must give their help to the work of the church'. Members of the congregation, he opined, 'still think that their whole duty to God and Christian society is done when they have been to church'! It was all too plain to him that, 'in far too many parishes the clergyman, with his wife, or his child, or his servant or someone connected with him, does all that is done'.[39] That said, by early 1860, when Wigram was appointed Bishop of Rochester, the situation had very much improved. At the seventh anniversary meeting in Winchester of the Hampshire Church School Society (which Wigram had helped to found), in June 1860, many positive notes were sounded. The Society now contained 230 names and the Revd Mr Mitchell, one of her Majesty's school inspectors, stated that 'at present the schools under inspection are mostly well built, well formed, well managed and cared for;

able teachers, ably assisted by competent pupil teachers, every year increase in number'.[40]

Wigram, by now Bishop of Rochester, had been invited back to share in the anniversary celebration. Many members of the Hampshire Church School Society and a large number of teachers were present at this big occasion, which included a service in the cathedral, a lecture, a conducted tour Winchester College and a social tea. They used the occasion to congratulate Wigram on his elevation to the See of Rochester and express their deep gratitude to him for his untiring work on behalf of the County's schools and education in general. The Dean of Winchester read an address in which he reminded those present of Wigram's remarkable achievements. As well as being the incumbent of one of the largest parishes in the country, he had 'afforded to us by God's grace, an example of the diligence, energy, and faithfulness which should distinguish the Christian pastor'. The Dean then added the following tribute.

> We desire to thank you again, as we have often done, for the many practical addresses delivered to us at your annual visitations; for your readiness to come among us, whether publicly or privately, when occasions arose requiring the presence of an official of the diocese; and especially this, that while discharging your archidiaconal duties, you exhibited the character of the Christian brother, and companion, and fellow labourer in the Gospel of Christ.
>
> While we ourselves have ever found you an able adviser in our difficulties, your repeated personal visits to our churches and parishes have been appreciated by the churchwardens of the Archdeaconry as well as ourselves.
>
> It was natural for us to expect in one who had been Secretary to the National Society a peculiar devotion to diocesan education— you have not disappointed these expectations.[41]

The Dean of Winchester's address was followed by another read by the Revd N. Midwinter on behalf of the undersigned Clergy, Patrons and Managers, Masters and Mistresses of Day Schools and Sunday School teachers in the Archdeaconry of Winchester.

> Venerable Sir—We, the undersigned … cannot permit you to leave this scene of your important Ministry without the expression of our heartfelt gratitude to Almighty God, and of thankfulness to

yourself, for zealous, affectionate and abundant labours which you have bestowed, during your period of office, on the education of the children in the Schools of Hampshire.

On your appointment to the Archdeaconry you did not fail to perceive that the cause of Day School Education was passing through a most important crisis, and that you could in no better way fulfil the duties of your high charge, and meet the expectation of the Lord Bishop of the Diocese, than by giving, as God might bless your efforts, a right direction to the energies which the movement had called forth.

The experience which your early labours as Secretary to the National Society brought to the counsels of the Diocesan Board of Education—the forethought which encouraged the formation of the Hampshire Church Schools Society, and the interest manifested in its continued prosperity, the energy which has led you to personal visitation more than once of, we believe, every Parish and Parochial School in the Archdeaconry—the munificence and zeal which have made your own large Parish of St. Mary, Southampton, with its School-houses rising up on every side, an example for similar efforts elsewhere—and, above all, the ready sympathy and kindness with which all your official duties have been discharged, have won for you personally our affectionate esteem, and have done much to secure for the Day Schools of Hampshire the eminent position which they have attained.[42]

Wigram was then thanked for helping to forward the Bishop's suggestions for Sunday Schools and Bible Classes 'by frequent attendance in all parts of the Archdeaconry, [at] those remarkable district meetings of Clergymen and Teachers and influential Laymen which have given such an impulse to these institutions.'[43] Remarkably the address which Midwinter finished reading had been signed by 1,630 noblemen, clergy, patrons and lay teachers.

OTHER EXTRA-PAROCHIAL CONCERNS

More locally *The Hampshire Chronicle* gave an account of the Anniversary of the Southampton District Association of the Society for the Propagation of the Gospel, which took place on Monday, 3 December 1855. The paper reported that the great and holy object of the Society

Joseph Cotton Wigram

was to provide the means to send out missionaries to the heathen of every land to assist in the fulfilment of the Divine command to the apostles. The meeting was chaired by Sir William Heathcote and Wigram was among those on the platform. It was pointed out 'that the Society was currently supporting 461 clergymen labouring throughout almost every part of the world to propagate the Gospel and uphold its glorious tenets'. Wigram took the chair at the evening meeting and urged that notwithstanding our many home-based commitments our hearts must always be open to the needs of those abroad.[44]

It is abundantly clear in all of this that Wigram exerted a huge amount of energy as he engaged in the various aspects of his ministry. In an age when few could see anything beyond the traditional parish unit with its tightly defined boundaries Wigram was able to think outside the box. With a steady resolve he restructured his very large and unwieldly parish creating smaller more manageable effective missional and community units. Each of these had their own designated and clearly defined boundaries and clergy who were adequately housed and financially supported. Wigram was also a conscientious pastor, who established an effective pastoral team. He was a dedicated teacher, who gave special attention to his confirmation candidates and the instruction of young people. He regularly visited the National and local schools in his home area. He gave particular attention to his preaching and published several sermons, among which were 'On Humility in the Hour of Success' and 'The Jews, The Appointed Witnesses for God in the Successive Ages of the World', which he preached on behalf of the Operative Jewish Converts' Institution at the Episcopal Chapel, Bethnal Green on 10 May 1855. Added to this he found time for writing. In the same year his book entitled *The Geography of the Holy Land* was reprinted. He had a continuing and passionate concern for education both within Southampton and wider environment of his Archdeaconry, which included the whole of the county of Hampshire and the Isle of Wight. Here he showed himself to be rightly aware and fully focused on the need for every parish and church to educate both the labouring and middle classes. Only in this way could the church grow and realise its calling to go into all the world and make disciples. In addition to these concerns by the year 1860 when Wigram left St Mary's there were nine children in the rectory ranging from Alfred the eldest, who was twenty-one, to Walter, who was just four years of age. One can only imagine with Wigram's strong advocacy of daily family prayer and Bible reading he maintained his household with a godly disciplined regime.

In his seminal work *Evangelicalism in Modern Britain*, David Bebbington identified four key characteristics of Evangelicalism, one of which was activism.[45] It was seen in 'seriousness', a 'strong sense of Ministerial obligation', 'laborious pastoral work', devotion to teaching, preaching and instruction and sheer hard work. In all his life and ministry Wigram fully illustrated this core aspect of Evangelicalism though he probably never reached the heights of his diocesan bishop Charles Sumner, who wrote more than 3,500 business letters in his last year of office.[46]

Surprisingly Wigram appears to have been in robust health and to have found time to engage in some devotional writing and study as well as taking part in the debates over several national issues including education and ritualism. It probably therefore came as no great surprise to the people of Southampton when they opened their copies of *The Hampshire Chronicle* on 28 April 1860, to read that the Chapter and officials of Rochester Cathedral had unanimously elected Wigram to become their next bishop in succession to the Right Revd George Murray, who had died having been in post for thirty-three years.[47]

Wigram preached his farewell sermons at St Mary's Church on the last Sunday of April 1860. In the morning he took his text from 1 Peter 2: 11, 'Dearly beloved, I beseech you as strangers and pilgrims, abstain from fleshly lusts, which war against your souls'.[48] He said that while he was anxious for the spiritual welfare of those committed to his care, he was by mysterious providence wrested from his usual course of labour, and, without any seeking of his own, he was exalted to a situation which required him to review the whole course of his ministerial life. In going on to review his time in St Mary's he saw it was chequered with trials and mercies, and that the trials had proved to be mercies in disguise.

In reflecting on Wigram's appointment to Rochester his diocesan bishop, Charles Sumner commented, 'It is more complimentary than convenient that the Crown can make no high appointment in the Church at home or abroad without a foray into my diocese. In the

Joseph Cotton Wigram

present instance my right arm is cut off to furnish Rochester with its chief ruler'.[49] Sumner expressed his confident hope that Wigram's episcopate would be of 'a most useful character'. He then went on to speak in terms of high praise of Wigram's ministry in his diocese.

> He is a very stirring man—full of energy and devotion to his work—and himself the foremost in setting an example of labour and self-denial in promoting it. I know few men more untiring in the discharge of *their proper duties* (a rare acquirement), or more efficient in performing them. I cannot doubt that he will carry a blessing with him.[50]

Notes

1. See Davies 1883, p. 343.
2. See St Mary's Church Wardens Book, 9 March 1851, SCA, MS PR5/6/4.
3. Statistics are from the 1851 census.
4. *Helps for the Pastoral Care of St Mary's*, Southampton, 1851, SCA, MS PR5/7/54.
5. Davies 1883, p. 351.
6. *Helps for the Pastoral Care of St Mary's Southampton*, 1851, SCA, MS PR5/7/54.
7. *The Hampshire Advertiser*, 10 June 1854.
8. Hansard, Third Series, CXXXIX, p. 500; quoted in Brose 1959, p. 185.
9. See for example Morris 1992, p. 122.
10. Mayor 1967, p. 9.
11. See Application for a new district to be called St Saviour's Bitterne, SCA, MS PR5/4/1/3.
12. J. C. Wigram, Application to establish a new district to be called St Luke, Newtown, 20 November 1851, SCA, MS PR5/4/1/4.
13. J. C. Wigram, Application to establish a new district to be called Bernard Street, 20 November 1851, SCA, MS PR5/4/1/15.
14. *Ibid.* Details of the Trinity district population are at the end.
15. Letter from the Ecclesiastical Commissioners, 20 December 1851, SCA, MS PR5/4/1/22.
16. J. Chalk, letter concerning Southampton Proposed Districts, 5 October 1852, SCA, MS PR5/4/1/39.
17. *Ibid.*
18. See Davies 1883, p. 343.
19. See J. C. Wigram, letter to John Murray, 16 September 1852, SCA, MS PR5/4/1/37.
20. Letter from Whitehall, 24 April 1853, SCA, MS PR5/4/1/50.
21. The *London Gazette*, 15 July 1859, p. 2752.
22. *Ibid.*

Rector of St Mary's, Southampton

23 St Mary's Church Wardens' Account Book, SCA, MS PR5/6/4.
24 Report of the Committee on the Repairs of St Mary's Church, 19 April 1851, SCA, MS PR5/7/3/5.
25 *The Hampshire Advertiser*, 2 March 1850.
26 Information from *To the Parishioners of St Mary's, Southampton*, 13 March 1853, SCA, MS PR5/7/78.
27 *Church Rates*, a flier, 1 March 1853, SCA, MS PR5/7/2/18.
28 *Ibid.*
29 Conveyance of land and Premises in Chapel Road, Southampton, for a National School, SCA, MS PR5/9/1/2.
30 J. G. Lonsdale, letter to Archdeacon Wigram, 27 December 1854, SCA, MS PR5/9/1/23.
31 *Ibid.*, 5 July 1858, SCA, MS PR5/6/4.
32 W. Churton, letter to Archdeacon Wigram, 2 January 1852, SCA, MS PR5/7/2/14.
33 I. Godden, letter to Archdeacon Wigram, 22 December 1857, SCA, MS PR5/7/2/12.
34 See J. C. Wigram, *A Letter on Sunday School Proceedings*, 1857, p. 3.
35 *Ibid.*, p. 6.
36 *Ibid.*, p. 19.
37 *Ibid.*, p. 17
38 *Ibid.*, p. 18.
39 J. C. Wigram, *A Charge ... 1855*, cited in appendix to *A Letter on Sunday School Proceedings ... 1857*, p. 23.
40 *The Hampshire Chronicle*, 2 June 1860.
41 This quotation, and others from the anniversary meeting are from *The Hampshire Chronicle*, 2 June 1860.
42 *The Hampshire Chronicle*, 2 June 1860.
43 *Ibid.*
44 *The Hampshire Advertiser*, 8 December 1855.
45 Bebbington 1989, pp. 10–12.
46 *Ibid.*, p. 11.
47 *The Hampshire Chronicle*, 28 April 1860.
48 *Ibid.*
49 Sumner 1876, p. 397.
50 *Ibid.*

5

Bishop of Rochester

Although Wigram's elevation to the episcopal bench came by invitation from the Prime Minister, Lord Palmerston, it very probably came about through the influence of the 7th Earl of Shaftesbury. Palmerston first became Prime Minister in 1855 and held office until 1858; in the following year he began a second term as Prime Minister, which lasted until July 1865. Palmerston had no religious enthusiasm and his Sunday church attendance was spasmodic at best. However, in 1839 at the age of fifty-four he married Lady Emily Cowper, who was the mother of Shaftesbury's wife Minnie. The Earl thus became Palmerston's step-son-in-law and a close relationship developed between the two men with Shaftesbury becoming a confidante. Shaftesbury reflected in 1865 that 'applicants, in abundant instances, approached the Prime Minster through me as their channel, and, as I never undertook any but deserving cases, so I never met with anything but ready acquiescence.'[1] When Palmerston first became Prime Minister Shaftesbury feared the worst and even wrote to his son Evelyn that 'he does not know in theology, Moses from Sydney Smith'.[2] However, he soon changed his mind when Palmerston became almost totally reliant on him in the matter of church appointments. The first bishops Palmerston appointed were decidedly of the Evangelical school with Shaftesbury noting in his diary 'my recommendations were made with that intention. I could not foresee the duration of his power, and I was resolved to put forward men who would preach the truth, be active in their diocese, be acceptable to the working people, and not offensive to the Nonconformists'.[3] When the See of Rochester became vacant in 1860 there was hardly anyone in England who matched those requirements better than Wigram. It should also be added that Wigram was well known to John Bird Sumner, the Archbishop of Canterbury, the elder brother of his Winchester diocesan bishop.

As soon as it was rumoured that Wigram was about to be appointed to Rochester local and national papers began to express their opinions on the matter. *The Times* trailed its bias: 'The Bishop nominated belongs to the Evangelical party, and since he has been at Southampton has shewn himself a determined opponent of horse-racing, theatrical entertainments, and friendly societies, all of which he has done much to suppress.'[4] *The Norfolk News* was among those more circumspect papers, commenting that Wigram 'is of the evangelical section of the Church, but moderate men of all parties would find little to object to in the appointment. The great evangelical societies will gain an accession of strength by this change of see.'[5] The evangelical paper, *The Record*, was not quite as enthusiastic as might have been expected: 'Other names will at once occur to which many of our readers might have given preference; but it will be generally allowed that the appointment is one which has at least this merit that moderate men of all parties will allow that it is unobjectionable.'[6] Notwithstanding such comments in the press Wigram's *alma mater*, Trinity College, Cambridge, wrote asking to honour him in the College Hall. Wigram replied that 'I shall be gratified by such distinction.'[7] Wigram's arms are emblazoned in the east window next to the bay window in the Hall.

The Hampshire Chronicle of 28 April 1860 reported that 'On Saturday last [21 April] a chapter of the prebends and other officials of Rochester Cathedral was held in the chapter-room of the cathedral, at twelve o'clock, for the purpose of electing a bishop, in obedience to her Majesty's *congé d'élire*,* in the place of the Hon. and Right Rev. George Murray, D.D., deceased, when the Revd Joseph Cotton Wigram, M.A., Archdeacon of Winchester, was unanimously elected to fill the vacant see. The deceased bishop held the see of Rochester for the long period

---

* *Congé d'élire*, Crown licence issued to the Dean and Chapter of a diocese authorising the election of a bishop: from the French *congé*, 'leave', and *élire*, 'to elect'.

of 33 years'.[8] The election was confirmed on the morning of Tuesday, 15 May. The preliminaries took place in the hall of the College of Advocates in London, where Wigram was received by the Vicar General of the Province of Canterbury and the Proctor for the Dean and Chapter of Rochester. After he had accepted the election and signed the schedule presented to him, he accompanied the Vicar General and other officials to the Church of St Mary-le-Bow in Cheapside, where prayers were said and the election was confirmed.[9]

Wigram's consecration took place on Thursday, 17 May in the parish church of St Mary, Lambeth, next door to Lambeth Palace, the Archbishop of Canterbury's London residence. Prayers were read by the Revd J. F. Lingham, the rector of Lambeth. After the sermon, Wigram, and the Revd William Jackson, who was consecrated to the bishopric of Antigua, were presented to the Archbishop and the consecration followed.[10] *The Kentish Observer* noted that the Bishop of Winchester was expected to be among the consecrating bishops.[11]

Wigram arrived in the city of Rochester on the evening of Saturday, 19 May having earlier done homage to the Queen. On the Sunday morning following he preached before the mayor and other dignitaries in the parish church of St Nicholas, taking as his text 1 Peter 2: 4–5 'To whom coming, as unto a living stone, disallowed indeed of men, but chosen by God and precious. Ye also, as lively stones are built up into a spiritual house, as an holy priesthood, to offer up spiritual sacrifices, acceptable to God by Jesus Christ'. He reminded the congregation that that the church is 'a spiritual building' raised on the rock which is Christ and built with living stones. 'The real disciples of Jesus', he stressed, 'were animated by a principle of life received from Him. He was the builder and they the living stones.' He went on to emphasise that 'St John says we shall be kings and priests with God and there is a ministry for everyone to perform in his own vocation'.[12]

Wigram's enthronement took place in the cathedral on the afternoon of Monday, 11 June in the presence of a large number of clergy and laity.[13] Before taking his seat on the throne he took the oaths of allegiance and abjuration as well as the oath to maintain the rights and privileges of the cathedral. It was noteworthy that he was the first bishop for many years not to have been enthroned by proxy. Wigram, it should be said, demonstrated his heart and sensitivity towards the poor by holding a special Sunday evening service the day before for the working classes, who had not been able to gain entry for the enthronement. His sermon was 'listened to with the most profound attention, and, from the earnest way in which it was delivered, created a deep impression'.[14]

EARLY DAYS IN THE DIOCESE

The diocese of Rochester had a long history dating back to its founding by St Augustine in 604 when, according to Bede, he consecrated Justus as its first bishop. In 1904 the Bishopric of Rochester provided an income of £4,000 per annum.[15] In early times the diocese consisted largely of the western part of Kent, which is believed to have been a separate sub-kingdom. But over time it expanded so that by the time of Wigram's arrival it included the deaneries of Rochester, Greenwich, Gravesend and Woolwich in Kent and the entire county of Hertford and almost all of Essex.[16] It also included parts of East London both north and south of the Thames. In 1864 it was reported that the diocese had a population of 608,000 people scattered over three counties with 601 legal benefices.[17] This meant that the bishop of Rochester was involved in a good deal of travel including back and forth across the Thames. Wigram based himself and his family at Danbury Palace in Essex (formerly Danbury Place), a modern Tudor-revival-style residence bought by the Church in 1845. But he also had a London home in Montague Place, Marylebone, where he often held meetings with clergy and where he stayed when he had business or confirmation services south of the river the following day. With a huge number clergy in his diocese Wigram's role of 'pastor pastorum' was inevitably going to prove demanding. *The Chelmsford Chronicle* of 28 December 1860 printed a free supplement listing all the significant public figures in Essex, and 'The List of Essex Clergy' alone, which included their places of residence, numbered just over six hundred.

Wigram realised the importance of making himself known and fairly soon after his arrival began to travel around in the diocese. The following visits, among the many he made, enable us to capture something of the energy and concern he had for those committed to his charge. At the beginning of June he visited Colchester and met with the mayor and town council. The mayor congratulated him on his appointment and the Revd L. R. Owen presented an address from the clergy of the rural deanery of Colchester. Wigram 'returned suitable replies and then proceeded to the 'Camp Church', where he confirmed 390 soldiers living in the camp.[18] Education was never far from Wigram's vision and agenda and on Monday, 11 June he presided over a meeting of supporters and teachers of Church of England Sunday School teachers. In his address, according to *The Rochester, Chatham and Strood Gazette*, 'the bishop shewed a hearty sympathy in the work, and an earnest desire to enlist the laity to take a prominent part in the religious training of the young'. At Wigram's request, the Revd A. Crowdy, who had been actively involved with him in the promotion of Sunday schools in the Winchester diocese, delivered 'a valuable address'. It was entitled 'On the Advantage to the Community of well-regulated Sunday Schools'. When Crowdy had finished speaking there was a unanimously supported resolution 'that an association be now formed of Church of England Sunday Schools for this part of the diocese; that the Right Reverend the Lord Bishop of Rochester be requested to be the President; that the committee be composed of such incumbents as shall connect their schools with the association, together with one layman for each school'. The meeting ended with expressions of thanks to Wigram for his part in the proceedings and his keen interest in Sunday schools.[19] On the evening of Wednesday, 8 August Wigram visited St George's Church, Gravesend. He arrived by train and was met by the churchwardens, the mayor and the corporation, the magistrates and many of the clergy of the town. A little later he was received at the church by the incumbent Revd Richard Joynes. Morning Prayer was read followed by Communion. Wigram took as the text for his sermon, Genesis 4: 9. 'And the Lord said unto Cain, "Where is thy brother?" And he said, "I know not; am I my brother's keeper?"' In the opinion of the local press it was a sermon which 'will long be remembered in Gravesend'—'a plain, practical statement of the relative duties of both the clergy and laity to each other, to the church, to the poor and the world outside'. A collection amounting to £50 12s. was made for the benefit of the infirmary and the National schools.[20] The bishop preached 'another excellent sermon' in the evening from Acts 20 :35 'It is more blessed to give than to receive'. On the following day, Thursday, 9 August, there was what a local paper described as 'an impressive re-opening of Strood Church' with the Bishop's presence drawing in 'a large crowd'. After prayers had been led by the Revd R. W. Shaw, Wigram read the Communion service in a very impressive manner and preached a sermon 'which was listened to with the greatest attention'. Perhaps unsurprisingly 'the offertory amounted to the liberal sum of £60 9s. and 6d'.[21]

By the early autumn it was evident to Wigram that the time was fast approaching when he would need to focus the minds of his diocesan clergy on his priorities and set out some clear objectives to be actioned. He therefore announced that he would hold his first Visitation in November.

WIGRAM'S STRATEGY FOR THE DIOCESE

Wigram's vision and strategy for the diocese is seen in many reports in local newspapers but most clearly in his two Charges delivered to the clergy and churchwardens at his general Visitations in November 1860 and November 1864. In both cases he began with some general remarks about the nature and state of affairs. At the time of his first Charge Wigram had only been in the diocese a matter of a few months and 'needed therefore a deeper insight'. It was therefore 'inexpedient', he said, 'to put before you any general admonitions or suggestions on those duties which are indispensable in our calling'.[22] He had, however, gained some insights through meetings he had held with rural deans. Wigram greatly valued the assistance of his fifty-one rural deans. He regarded them as his eyes and ears and made a pledge to visit all their rural deaneries before the time of his second his next triennial Visitation. *The Chelmsford Chronicle* carried reports of two such meetings held in the deaneries of Dengie and Bradwell-on-Sea. At the latter the bishop dined with the clergy and wardens and a number of issues were discussed.[23] *The Hertford Mercury and Reformer* of 26 October published details of a forthcoming series of local conferences which Wigram would be arranging with the help of rural deans. These would enable the clergy to consider and discuss the issues which he would be setting out in his first Visitation. The schedule captures something of the demands made on Wigram. The dates were as follows:

> Thursday November 7th Southend; Monday 11th at Brentwood; Wednesday 20th Rochester; Monday 25th at Saffron Walden; Wednesday 27th at Chelmsford; Thursday 28th Halstead; Friday 29th at Colchester; Monday December 2nd Hertford; Wednesday 4th St Albans; Thursday 5th Hitchin; Friday 6th Bishop Stortford; Monday 6th at Maldon.[24]

Wigram took care over his senior appointments, one of the earliest being that of the Revd Joseph B. McCaul as his chaplain. With his strong evangelical convictions McCaul was a man after Wigram's own heart. He was curate of St Edmund the King in Lombard Street, London. He was also an assistant librarian at the British Museum and a former Divinity Lecturer at King's College, London, and had prepared Charles Simeon's *Horae Homileticae* for publication. He shared Wigram's distaste for Bishop Colenso's radical interpretations of the Old Testament and wrote ten critical letters against him in *The Record*.[25] In 1864 Wigram appointed William Brice Ady (1816–82), rector of Little Baddow, as Archdeacon of Colchester and he proved to be a solid and supportive colleague.[26] Wigram also expressed his great indebtedness to Ady's predecessor, Charles Parr Burney (1786–1864), 'for the leading role which he had always taken in the religious work of the county in promoting good feeling among clergy and laity'.[27] At the time of his second Visitation Wigram acknowledged the counsels of his three archdeacons.[28] At the time of his second Visitation Wigram was able to present some definite some diocesan facts and figures. On average there were about 900 souls in each parish. He was encouraged that 240 curates were helping incumbents, 'but regretted that 60, one tenth of our incumbents, have been more or less non-resident this last year'.[29] The total number of worshippers on the Lord's day is reported as, morning, 138,328; afternoon, 152,995.[30]

Joseph Cotton Wigram

CLERGY AND LAITY WORKING TOGETHER

Inevitably the heart and core of Wigram's strategy was dependent on the roles of both the clergy and laity working together in a common cause. He was acutely aware that too many clergy were living in isolation from the people they were called to serve. 'The Pastor', he emphasised, 'requires help from those among whom he labours.' Significantly Wigram sub-titled his first Visitation, 'Fellowship with the Flock essential to the true Pastoral System'. He had observed from the reports of the rural deans 'a wish on the part of many clergy to draw nearer in fellowship with the laity' and 'to receive more freely their counsels and co-operation'. There is Wigram emphasised 'a yearning amongst the Laity to work on behalf of the Church of which they are living members'.[31]

Coming fresh from organising his large parish in Southampton, Wigram knew the great value and importance of lay ministries. In his Primary Charge of 1860, he stressed the effectiveness of the Scripture reader, the town-missionary, the book-hawker and the tract distributor. He was particularly full of praise for Scripture readers and their work in the parishes. 'It is', he said, 'no light service which some gentlemen in this diocese do, who attend at an out-door room provided for their gardening and farming men to take their meals in.' 'And there', he continued, 'at the breakfast hour, read a few verses of Scripture, accompanied by a word of suitable comment, before offering the morning prayer.'[32] Wigram was also so greatly impressed by the value of 'Book-Hawking' that he made it the third sub-heading in his 1864 Visitation Charge. He pointed out that 'six hawkers have been diligently at work, having made in less than a year two or three visits to every parish, where they called at most houses throughout the villages, and sold 1,555 Bibles, 5,824 Common Prayer Books, and a vast number of miscellaneous tracts and prints at a cost of £1,086 2s. 7d.'. Wigram stressed that their work was a great supplement to schoolteachers, and it had also helped to satisfy a growing need for books.[33] These lay ministries had the effect of deepening the combination between the laity and clergy. 'Foreigners', Wigram asserted, 'regard them with astonishment, as the peculiarity and glory of our land'![34]

Bishop of Rochester

It seems that not everyone was quite so impressed by Wigram's fulsome praise of the clergy and laity working together within his diocese. In January 1865 *The Chelmsford Chronicle* published some correspondence between Wigram and Lord Ebury. The latter gentleman asserted that the laity were still over-looked and that reform was still needed in the church at large. 'A new code embodied in act of Parliament', he asserted, 'should provide that clergy accused of immorality must be tried by the ordinary courts of justice.' He went on to reiterate that the law 'must give parishioners and congregations some power of dealing with those incumbents—of which, unfortunately, we are not without examples—who are unable to comprehend their responsibilities'. Ebury had plenty more to say including that 'the liturgy and rubrics must be revised, so as to get rid of those many unmeaning, tedious, formalising repetitions ... which have much to do with keeping our worshippers from the Lord's table'. Regarding the baptism service, Ebury bemoaned that it is 'unnecessarily long' and had resulted in 'centuries of controversy' with opposing parties 'still as far as ever from an agreement as to the meaning'. Lord Ebury concluded stating, 'For myself, my Lord, so long as I can entertain the least hope of the reformation of our church, I shall cling to her'.[35] The following week the *Chronicle* did its best to defend Wigram in a long article with citations from Wigram's Charge. Among the points raised the paper underlined that the clergy were never more focused on their ministries 'and held in so high esteem as now'. Men being trained for the ministry at King's College, London were of high quality and the number of clergy serving London parishes was greatly increased. The article also drew attention to Wigram's statistics of the contribution of the laity in his diocese. In addition to 1,146 church wardens, there were 1,190 parish visitors (119 males and 991 females), with 3,254 voluntary Sunday school teachers (1,003 males and 2,251 females).[36]

Just three months before his death Wigram was still strongly focused on the importance of the role of the laity if churches were to grow and the message of the Gospel extended. In January 1867 *The Essex Weekly News* published at his request the report of a meeting of the sub-committee appointed by the three conferences of clergy and laity held during the course of autumn at Hertford, Chelmsford and Southend 'to find improved ways for securing the assistance of the laity in parochial work'.[37] They agreed two resolutions unanimously, namely:

> 1. That this meeting concurs in the opinion that it will be for the advantage of the Church in this diocese that the clergy should invite the increased co-operation of the laity for the parishes in spiritual as well as temporal matters; and that such co-operation will be greatly promoted if it shall receive the formal sanction of the bishop of the Diocese.
> 2. That the meeting is further of the opinion that the following are some of the methods in which the laity may co-operate with, and materially assist, the clergy in their duties.[38]

Twelve suggested methods were listed. They included 'teaching' in Sunday and night schools; 'visiting', including the poor, the sick, workhouses, union houses and hospitals; 'distributing Christian literature', including Bibles and Prayer Books; 'conducting church services' in school rooms and cottages; giving lectures in both towns and rural communities and managing and assisting in the running of Working Men's Societies, Penny Banks, Post Office Savings Banks, and Clothing and Providential Institutions. Wigram attached a brief comment at the end of his circular commending the resolutions and expressing his earnest hope that it would result in 'the cordial co-operation of the laity and clergy' and be the subject of frequent and fervent prayer'.[39]

Wigram was also a great advocate of the role of women and pioneered the development of their ministry within a parish setting. In his first Charge he reminded clergy of the important role accorded to women both young and old in the Epistles to Timothy and Titus. He also added:

> We find that Phoebe, "a sister", and "the servant of the Church" had business to do which was likely to need the help of other saints. She is described as having been a "succourer of many", and of Paul himself. Mary "had bestowed much labour on him, and on those with him", Tryphena and Tryphosa, with the beloved Persis, had "laboured in the Lord", the latter "much". Others were "helpers in Christ Jesus", and "laboured in the Gospel" with the Apostle.[40]

And, having been in the diocese for several years, he declared, 'I cannot withhold an expression of my deep conviction, that in very many parts of the diocese we need a considerable female agency,—mission women, and such like female helpers as have been brought to bear in other parts for relieving sorrows, and checking the grosser habits of their own sex'. 'They are', Wigram opined, 'invaluable aids to a clergyman.'[41]

Coupled with his insistence on lay ministry Wigram felt it necessary to stress to his clergy in 1864 the great importance of their parishes being generally missionary orientated. It was his view that every pastor should ensure that his people are interested in missionary work abroad. Interest in overseas missions he believed, caused people to think more of the people at home.[42] He estimated that in only 327 out the 600 parishes in the diocese was there any support for home missions and it was only marginally better where foreign missions were concerned.[43]

At a number of area-clergy meetings he recommended the Society for the Propagation of the Gospel (SPG) and the Church Missionary Society (CMS).[44] Wigram's parents, and other family members, had been supporters of the CMS and it occupied a special place in his heart. Speaking at its thirty-sixth Annual General Meeting, he recounted that the society had been in existence for sixty years. After the first twenty years the society employed sixteen English clergymen and no native clergy at all. Now, however, it had 'not fewer than 179 English clergymen and fifty-nine ordained native missionaries'. He went on to say, that 'as long as he had continued strength of body and mind, nothing should be wanting on his part in the way doing everything he possibly could to support the society'.[45] Wigram preached a sermon in Winchester in November 1849 to mark the Jubilee of the Church Missionary Society.[46] In it he recounted the growing progress of the Christian gospel in New Zealand through the labours of Samuel Marsden. He underlined the importance of imposing western values and culture on the indigenous peoples. He urged

> Civilization is advancing; European dress, and habits, and customs, are being rapidly adopted; the tillage of the ground, and the methods which we follow in preparing food, and overcoming natural difficulties, are being practised. The wandering, thievish, and evil customs of the people are giving way; the superstitions and delusions by which they have been led astray are dispelled by the

> light of the truth, and sound principles of reason, and the correct
> methods of thought which are familiar to us in Christendom, are
> being learnt by them:—they are themselves being "Christified".[47]

This imposing of Western Christian values on indigenous peoples, which Wigram and indeed the CMS articulated, was a basic in much of nineteenth-century mission strategy. In New Zealand it brought peace and reconciliation to warring factions, an intense love for the observance of the Sabbath day, a desire on the part of both children and chiefs to be taught and the cessation of many savage customs. In the light of this transformation Wigram urged that this is a cause worthy of our help. He concluded, 'Freely you have received, freely give; that the word of the Lord may have free course and be glorified; that souls may be saved; that by turning many to righteousness, you yourselves may shine like stars, for ever and ever'.[48]

In regards to home missions Wigram commended the work of The Additional Curates' Aid Society and chaired their meeting held on the 25 October 1860. He 'expressed the hope that the society would continue to prosper so as to meet the demands upon its funds'.[49] In March 1863 Wigram issued his annual appeal to clergy to preach sermons on behalf of home and foreign missions. His choice of home mission was The Incorporated Church Building Society in London, the sermon to be preached between Easter and Trinity Sunday. For the foreign mission Wigram selected either the SPG or the CMS, or any other foreign missionary society connected with the Church of England, the sermons and collections to be made between Advent and Epiphany'.[50]

On the matter of clergy income in 1864 Wigram had ascertained that in 181 benefices it was less than £200 per year and in some instances was as little as £75. This was a great hindrance and all the poorer livings would be raised to £200. The average pay for curates in the diocese was just below £100 but with a house rarely found. He also expressed his satisfaction that some of the non-university curates serving in the diocese were proving to be 'very efficient and competent pastors'. Some who had previously served in the army and navy had brought their discipline and gentlemanly bearing to the sacred cause. This must have been particularly pleasing since he had earlier expressed his disapproval of his clergy becoming members of cricket teams or archery or modern rifle clubs. He also warned of the dangers of 'the card table, or the ballroom, the theatre or opera, hunting, shooting, or any field sports'. If these are the outlets, though lawful, that occupy a young clergyman's time, 'they will tend to obscure the difference between true religion and the system of the world'. Wigram also counselled clergy to avoid 'a taste for dress' and 'the refinements of the drawing room which characterise the men of the world in our time'. He further added that 'the practice of smoking, which is condemned by medical authorities for men in health, or the cultivation of an inordinate profusion of hair about the face, which is forbidden in the British Camp and may well be omitted by the soldier of Christ, distinguishing such persons generally'.[51] Another concern was that of clergymen who combined secular work with their religious duties. This matter came to the fore over the Revd George Davies of Ingatestone, who was earning his living as a farmer but also gaining additional income by taking on occasional Sunday duties. Wigram wrote a disapproving letter to the press about Davies' behaviour.[52] In the process he inadvertently offended some of the Essex farmers, who mistakenly felt he was disparaging of their occupation. One of their number, Charles G. Round, wrote to *The Chelmsford Chronicle* advising that it would be helpful if Wigram could clarify the matter. This he did in a most gracious manner.[53]

CHURCH BUILDING AND PROPERTY

Wigram was concerned over the poor state of a good many church buildings within the diocese and the low level at which some clergy were paid. In the spring of 1863, the Archdeacon of Hertfordshire reported that 'above twenty of our 163 churches still require extensive reparation and proportionate outlay'. The Archdeacon of Essex offered a similar story. 'We still have a good deal of work before us. Only 90 churches in the two archdeaconries have as yet received assistance from the diocesan society, and its income remains miserably small.'[54] In view of this Wigram urged patrons of livings and owners of land to look to the needs of church property and facilities and to ensure that there was proper management. In particular, he stressed that rents from glebe and other church lands and property must be collected in full. The income thus raised could be put towards building repairs and maintenance. In the spring of 1863 Wigram issued an appeal to all his clergy informing them of 'the need of continued aid in the work of church building'.

SACRAMENTS

Despite being dubbed an extreme low churchman by the High Church press, Wigram impressed on his clergy the importance of the sacraments of baptism and the Lord's Supper. Baptisms, he declared, should be taking place 'in the midst of the congregation' and on a fixed Sunday each month. Such was the practice in 423 churches in the diocese but not in the case of 221. He hoped to see every parish adopting this custom, indeed, he was adamant that 'It is most important that this practice should be observed'. He regarded baptism as 'a memento' to every man of his profession.

Wigram made it clear that celebrating Holy Communion less than one Sunday a month was insufficient. When he first arrived in the diocese 270 of parishes held Communion services less than 12 times a year. Of those 270, four churches kept the sacrament only four times or less during the year.[55] By the time of his second Visitation in 1864 Wigram was pleased to report that the situation was much improved, there now being 470 churches where Communion services were held twelve times a year or more.[56] He urged his clergy to make sure that the subjects of baptism and confirmation featured in their Sunday sermons. In addition, there should always be an ongoing class in each parish preparing people for confirmation. He reminded them that confirmation services were held in major towns across the diocese each spring and that he would be ready to confirm at any time where a sufficient number of candidates had been prepared.[57]

Bishop of Rochester

A GOSPEL FOR THE POOR

Having had a long parochial ministry in London, East Tisted and at St Mary's in Southampton, Wigram was very personally aware of the needs of both the urban and the rural poor. He would also have been acutely aware that the message that Jesus came to bring was one of 'good news to the poor' and that the Apostle Paul had spent much time raising sums of money for the needs of the poor in Jerusalem and elsewhere. Indeed, Wigram himself frequently preached sermons on behalf of charities and benefit institutions. Speaking in 1860 he endorsed the views of a fellow bishop, who had stated, 'Here surely has been one of the church's great errors, which has drawn down its appropriate punishment; that she has neglected to provide work for those whose consciences told them they ought to work'. 'To aid the poor', Wigram asserted, 'is often the first step of vital religion.' He pointed out that in many parishes in the diocese the poor had been neglected and in consequence many of the 'most earnest of our flocks' had been carried off into other communions. He was doubtless aware of the growing strengths of the Primitive Methodists in Essex and Hertfordshire, who were pulling the working poor into their congregations in significant numbers. Wigram therefore spoke in forthright terms urging clergy 'not to be afraid of doing something for God among the poor'. In November 1861 he called together a conference of clergy and laity at Chelmsford to discuss 'The present state of the Labouring Classes, their circumstances, peculiar temptations, domestic and social occupations, &c., &c., with the best methods of improving their material, social and religious condition'.[58] He followed this with a similar gathering at Maldon in Essex attended by 150 clergy and laity, when 'the condition of the labouring classes' was discussed.[59] *The Chelmsford Chronicle* reported that the Lord Bishop, who presided, stated that this was 'the last conference of the series' and that he had received positive satisfaction from those who had attended the earlier meetings.[60] Significantly in his closing remarks Wigram observed that 'this was the first meeting at which they had had the presence of ladies. He welcomed them, and said how much better [and] frequently they could do things for the poor, and did, than men could'.[61] In April 1863 *The Chelms-*

Joseph Cotton Wigram

ford Chronicle reported that 'the first of a series of special services to the working classes was held on Thursday evening, the 16th inst., at St. James' Church, Colchester, when the Revd Charles Burney, MA, vicar of Halsted, and chaplain to the Bishop of Rochester, preached an impressive sermon from 1st Timothy i, 15'. It continued, 'we understand that similar services are intended to be held at most of the churches in the town during the spring'.[62]

Among the poor. Wigram expressed his particular concern for incumbents on very low incomes and clergy widows. He announced the setting up of a new fund for the relief of the families of 'that portion of our brotherhood who possess the least share of worldly means'. The fund is 'designed to lessen materially the expenses of life assurance, and to provide against sufferings, often most intense, of widows and orphans of Clergy, (whether Incumbents or Curates) when removed by the providence of God from this world'.[63]

Addressing his clergy three years later Wigram sounded an altogether more positive note. He spoke of 'Christian benevolence breaking out' and of the added strength which flowed from 'our provident institutions and savings' banks (so greatly improved by the post-office agency) which should be commended and made known, and all our well-conducted village clubs, our dispensaries infirmaries and hospitals'.[64] He was particularly pleased at the reports which had reached him from some of the chief societies which operated with the diocese. He knew of no more successful efforts than those made among the sailors and soldiers at Gravesend and Chatham. The Medway branch of the Mission to Seamen Afloat and The Waterside Mission at Gravesend were 'full of usefulness'. That said, Wigram was troubled by the behaviour of the soldiers at Colchester and 'the prevalence of drinking and immoralities'.[65] In January 1867 he was evidently still concerned about the needs of the poor and sent out a circular to all his clergy urging them to encourage the members of their congregations to visit and make contact with working-class men and women in their neighbourhood. He felt this was particularly urgent in those parts of the diocese where there are 'factories for silk, paper, & co., our straw-plaiting districts; our brick-makers, chalk, cement and pottery workers—especially along the Thames and Medway; the bargemen and watermen; the low islanders from Canvey to Foulness and the rural agricultural places throughout the diocese'.⁶⁶

Wigram stressed that it was vital that churches should be making a practical impact on society and the poor in particular. It is part of the way in which the Kingdom of God is helped forward. He reminded clergy that the Lord Jesus himself stressed this same principle.

> Are any hungry or thirsty? Are any sick or in prison?—to whom does he look to visit and relieve such? Not assuredly, to the ministers and preachers of the word only, but to everyone who lives, or hopes to live, through the gospel; to each and all of those to whom He will say in the great day, 'Inasmuch as ye have done it, or done it not, unto one of the least of these my brethren, ye have done it unto me'. Yes, *that* is 'pure religion and undefiled before God and the Father', which impels him who possesses it, to 'visit, not by deputy, but his own person, the fatherless and widows in their affliction, as well as keep himself unspotted from the world', And it is the peculiar triumph of Christianity, that it not only disposes a man to such services, but fits him for them.⁶⁷

Lest anyone should be concerned that charitable work might be hindrance to the quality of their spiritual well-being, Wigram countered by saying he who follows this course of practical caring action 'derives himself the greatest spiritual benefit from it ... To faith and love thus put forth in action God will add the graces of inward peace and joy'.⁶⁸ He summed up this matter of practical care for the poor and marginalised by stressing that only when every Christian member is working together for the good of others will the body of Christ be in good health.⁶⁹

A mark of Wigram's spiritual concern for the working poor was his publication in 1862 of *The Cottager's Daily Family Prayers*.⁷⁰ Despite his enormous workload and constant travel in his expansive diocese, the needs of the poor were never far from Wigram's heart and he still found time to produce this twenty-three page pamphlet to help and encourage those on the margins of society to build a spiritual life. It begins with an extract from a printed farewell sermon on his leaving his curacy at Leytonstone on the 27 April 1827.

> I know nothing, among domestic duties, so calculated to bring the blessing of GOD ALMIGHTY upon you and yours as that of FAMILY PRAYER ... I would that in every house and cottage of this place,

> there should be some time, morning or evening... when parents, with their children, and every person who is in the house, should assemble together...that one of them should read a proper form of prayer, and all the other follow him, with their lips, thoughts and hearts,—this done, that all should repeat the Lord's Prayer aloud together—and then close their devotions with the blessing.[71]

Wigram's booklet is carefully geared to the needs of those who had only a minimal formal education. There is a very short devotion for each day focused on an aspect of holy living, and a brief prayer on the theme, which includes the needs of the family. For example, on Tuesday night's the devotional is 'Fruits of the Spirit' and the prayer, 'that we may be delivered from vain and bad desires, from sinful words and unholy thoughts'.[72] Other themes include 'Peace in Believing' on Wednesday, 'The Family of Christ' on Thursday, and 'Self-Denial' for Friday.[73]

EDUCATION

For almost all his life and ministry Wigram had been engaged and absorbed in issues relating to education. During his years at Westminster he had been General Secretary of the National Society and had written books on the education of children. In his years as incumbent of the rural living of East Tisted and the urban parish of St Mary's Southampton and as Archdeacon of Winchester, schools in the county of Hampshire had been a significant and major concern. It is no surprise that on coming to Rochester as the new bishop he soon turned his focus to the educational needs of his diocese. Just days after his arrival Wigram paid his first visit to Hertford and preached what *The Chelmsford Chronicle* described as 'an able sermon at All Saints' Church on behalf of the Herts. Boards of Education'. It was based on Galatians 6: 7–8, 'Be not deceived; God is not mocked; for whatever a man sows, that shall he also reap'. He urged on all his hearers the duty and responsibility of efforts to promote the proper training of the young, on the ground that the character of the individual was 'influenced and determined by his early training, and his everlasting destiny fixed and decided by his habits and conduct here'.[74] At a public meeting held after lunch, Wigram referred to the county from which he had just come and went on to commend the value of detailed inspections of teaching and 'to deplore the early age at which children left school'. The proceedings ended with the High Sheriff's resolution, 'That this meeting desires to express its grateful acknowledgments to the Lord Bishop of the diocese for attending upon the present occasion, and advocating the cause of the board in the pulpit'.[75] Wigram, it should be said, set a very high value on thorough schools' inspections. In the spring of 1861, he appointed a number of diocesan school inspectors and met with them at his London home to assign them to particular districts. When their work was completed, he met with them at his Danbury residence on the 7 and 8 August 'for mutual counsel and confidential conference with their Diocesan on the important duties of their office'.[76]

Although *Hansard* cannot be guaranteed to record every speech made in Parliament, there is only one instance recorded of Wigram having spoken in the House of Lords—on 5 June 1862. Significantly it concerned education and the interaction between the Committee of the Privy Council and the Committee of National Society. A local group in the parish of Chrishall in his diocese had applied for a grant from the Committee of the Privy Council to build a school which would be under the National Society. The application had been refused on the ground that half the residents were dissenters, who would not wish their children to have religious education in the proposed school with a Church of England bias. The dissenters, however, joined the church people and requested that this difficulty could be waived. However, the Privy Council took the view that although the existing Nonconformist parishioners might be happy future Nonconformists might not feel the same way. Wigram argued that 'it was not correct that there was anything of a proselytising character in the National Society, beyond that which must necessarily belong to it as a representative of the Church of England'. He also suggested that the school managers' 'discretionary powers to investigate cases of proselytising or abuse should be a sufficient safeguard to the consciences of dissenting parents'. Wigram therefore put forward the motion that this be a matter for further debate. His motion was supported by Lord Redesdale and the Bishops of Lincoln and Llandaff, the latter stating that if the matter complained of by his friend the Bishop of Rochester became general, 'they would have no schools at all in our small rural parishes, and that the complaint that those parishes were neglected would go unredressed'.[77]

Addressing the clergy in November 1860 at his first Visitation and Charge to the clergy Wigram brought their attention to 'a vast amount of good I have seen accomplished by the Laity as Sunday School Teachers (elderly, middle-aged, and youthful persons alike) and as Superintendents of Sunday Schools'. He also underlined the effective service being done by so many teachers in day schools and evening classes and went on to demonstrate how ordinary people can create significant learning opportunities. He cited the case of four Hampshire farmers, who read with their labourers for an hour every Sunday evening, and the son of another, who taught the ploughboys in the stable during their dinner hour.[78]

Wigram revisited education at the time of his second Visitation in 1864 as one of the significant issues calling for attention. He began by speaking of the increasingly strained relationship between the church and state in the matter of education. In particular, he referred to the requirement that in new schools funded by the government religious teaching should be objective and the Bible not interpreted in accord with any denominational doctrine. This state of affairs had come about owing to the growing impact of Nonconformist parents publicly objecting to Church of England doctrine being taught to their children albeit in Church of England schools. This meant that the National Society had been forced to new terms when seeking government funding for particular schools. The Committee of the Privy Council's refusal to grant government financial aid for a school in the parish of Chrishall brought to a head the issue that Wigram had been challenging since his time as General Secretary of the National Society in the 1830s. He fully recognised the feelings of the dissenters in this matter, but he believed the government was using them as a means to secularise the education in the nation's schools.

On a positive note, however, Wigram took great satisfaction over the accomplishments of the new diocesan training college at Hockerill in Hertfordshire, where students were prepared as teachers for National Church of England schools. Because of the liberalising of religious education Wigram urged that Sunday schools 'give increased diligence in inculcating the principles of Christ as held by the Church'.[79]

DIOCESAN ADMINISTRATION

Few can doubt that bishop Wigram was indeed an extremely able, conscientious and effective diocesan administrator. He was constantly on the move, journeying throughout the length and breadth of a large and straggling See, which included the western half of Kent, traversed the Thames, included parts of north-east and south-east London and covered the whole of Hertfordshire and most of Essex.

Wigram understood the importance of making his presence widely known and made it his business to chair both church and public meetings whenever possible. That said, it is clear from press reports that he leant a good deal on his Archdeacons for advice on matters both temporal and spiritual. He made widespread and frequent use of his rural deans, who organised frequent area meetings, many of which he then chaired. Wigram, as has been seen in this chapter, was a good listener and the many meetings which were organised across his diocese became forums for debate and hearing the views of his clergy. Major decisions were agreed, and resolutions made as the basis for ongoing or future action.

On his arrival in the diocese in 1860 he had called together all his rural deans in order to ascertain from them the most pressing needs and the conditions within the diocese. He later wrote that it was the character of their reports that prompted him to advocate and promote a closer fellowship between the clergy and the laity.[80] In 1861 he also set himself the task of visiting all his fifty rural deaneries during the next two years.[81] Wigram's commitment to collaborative decision making was particularly well seen in a whole series of clergy conferences, which he held in various parts of the diocese to give further consideration to the issues that he had raised at his triennial Visitations. The major focus of those gatherings centred on giving, mission work, holding firm to the doctrines of the Gospel, the spiritual improvement of a country parish, especially as regards to frequent communions, the social and moral condition of the agricultural worker, the book-hawker's work, village and Sunday schools and Harvest Homes.[82]

One of the great strengths of Wigram's diocesan strategy and organisation was that having listened carefully to both clergy and laity and reflecting on his past experience he ascertained the essential and crucial needs of the diocese. First, there was the need for clergy to work together with the laity, including women, taking on new and growing roles. Second, Wigram was acutely conscious of the necessity to support and develop education at every level. He was particularly concerned that so many children were leaving school at the age of ten. He therefore constantly urged the need for more church schools at every level from Children's Sunday schools to adult evening classes. More and better trained teachers and properly inspected schools were to be a vital part of this process. Third, Wigram had a deep concern for the needs of the poor. Throughout his whole ministry he had been surrounded by the poor and marginalised. He clearly felt compelled to keep their needs constantly before the people of his diocese. On a number of occasions his clergy were asked to consider 'The present state of the labouring classes, their circumstances, peculiar temptations, domestic and social occupations, ordinary recreations, &c., with the best methods of improving their material, social and religious condition'.[83] Fourth, and not quite as high in profile, were the needs of the clergy and church property. Wigram was particularly concerned that clergy should have sufficient income to live adequately and that the building in which they led worship should be in good condition and well maintained. When Wigram died, unexpectedly in April 1867, there were few indeed who did not know the things which mattered most to him and there were probably not many who would have disagreed with him.

Notes

[1] Hodder 1886, vol. 3, p. 191.
[2] *Ibid.*, vol. 2, p. 505.
[3] *Ibid.*, vol. 3, p. 197.
[4] *The Sherborne Mercury*, 27 March 1860.
[5] *The Norfolk News*, 7 April 1860.
[6] *The Record*, 23 March 1860.

Bishop of Rochester

7 J. C. Wigram, letter to the Master of Trinity College, Cambridge, 14 November 1860, Trinity College Archives, Add. MS c. 9181.
8 *The Hampshire Chronicle*, 28 April 1860.
9 *The Rochester, Chatham and Strood Gazette*, 22 May 1860.
10 Ibid.
11 *The Kentish Observer*, 17 May 1860.
12 *The Rochester, Chatham and Strood Gazette*, 22 May 1860.
13 Ibid., 12 June 1860.
14 *The Chelmsford Chronicle*, 15 June 1860.
15 Blackie 1948, p. 539 (entry for the See of Rochester).
16 Ibid.
17 J. C. Wigram, *A Charge . . . 1864*, p. 2.
18 *The Rochester, Chatham and Strood Gazette*, 5 June 1860.
19 Ibid., 1 June 1860.
20 Ibid., 14 August 1860.
21 Ibid.
22 J. C Wigram, *A Charge . . . 1860*, p. 4.
23 *The Chelmsford Chronicle*, 11 January 1861.
24 *The Hertford Mercury and Reformer*, 2 October 1861.
25 *The Kentish Gazette*, 31 July 1860; *Crockford's Clerical Directory*, 1865.
26 *The Kentish Gazette*, 22 November 1864; *Crockford's Clerical Directory*, 1865. See also *Alumni Oxonienses . . . 1715–1886*.
27 See obituary, 'The Late Archdeacon Burney', in *The Essex Weekly News*, 11 November 1864.
28 *The Chelmsford Chronicle*, 3 February 1865.
29 J. C. Wigram, *A Charge . . . 1864*, p. 4.
30 Ibid., p. 8.
31 J. C Wigram, *A Charge . . . 1860*, p. 7.
32 Ibid., p. 19.
33 J. C Wigram, *A Charge . . . 1864*, pp. 14–15.
34 J. C. Wigram, *A Charge . . . 1860*, p. 7.
35 Lord Ebury, letter to the Bishop of Rochester, 18 January 1865, in *The Chelmsford Chronicle*, 27 January 1865.
36 *The Chelmsford Chronicle*, 3 February 1865.
37 *The Essex Weekly News*, 25 January 1867.
38 Ibid.
39 Ibid.
40 J. C. Wigram, *A Charge . . . 1860*, p. 13.
41 J. C. Wigram, *A Charge . . . 1864*, p. 19.
42 *The Chelmsford Chronicle*, 5 April 1861. The paper gave extended coverage of the CMS AGM.

43 J. C. Wigram, *A Charge ... 1864*, p. 34.
44 J. C. Wigram, *A Charge ... 1860*, p. 31.
45 *Ibid.*
46 J. C. Wigram, *A Jubilee Retrospect. Five Sermons*, 1849. Wigram preached Sermon V on New Zealand.
47 *Ibid.*, pp. 98–9.
48 *Ibid.*, p. 109.
49 *Supplement to the Chelmsford Chronicle*, 2 November 1860.
50 *The Chelmsford Chronicle*, 13 March 1863.
51 J. C. Wigram, *A Charge ... 1860*, pp. 22–4.
52 See *The Chelmsford Chronicle*, 29 May 1863.
53 *Ibid.*, 27 June 1863.
54 *Ibid.*, 13 March 1863.
55 J. C. Wigram, *A Charge ... 1864*, p. 10.
56 *Ibid.*
57 *Ibid.*
58 *The Chelmsford Chronicle*, 13 March 1863.
59 *Ibid.*, 20 December 1861.
60 *Ibid.*, 27 December, 1861.
61 *Ibid.*
62 *Ibid.*, 24 April 1863.
63 J. C. Wigram, *A Charge ... 1860*, p. 5.
64 *Ibid.*
65 J. C. Wigram, *A Charge ... 1860*, pp. 17–19.
66 *The Essex Weekly News*, 25 January 1867.
67 J. C. Wigram, *A Charge ... 1860*, p. 11.
68 *Ibid.*
69 *Ibid.*, p. 12.
70 J. C. Wigram, *The Cottager's Daily Family Prayers*, 1862.
71 *Ibid.*, Introduction.
72 *Ibid.*, p. 13.
73 *Ibid.*, pp. 15, 17 and 19.
74 *The Chelmsford Chronicle*, 8 June 1860.
75 *Ibid.*
76 *Ibid.*, 16 August 1861.
77 *Hansard*, Third Series, CLXVII, pp. 400–7.
78 J. C. Wigram, *A Charge ... 1860*, p. 19.
79 J. C. Wigram, *A Charge ... 1864*, p. 50.
80 J. C. Wigram, *A Charge ... 1860*, p. 6.
81 *The Chelmsford Chronicle*, 11 January 1863.

[82] J. C. Wigram, *A Charge ... 1860*, pp. 29–30.
[83] See for example *The Hertford Mercury and Reformer*, 26 October 1861.

6

Doubt, Ritualism and Bishop Colenso

Outwardly speaking, the middle years of Victorian England were regarded by many as a period of confidence. The 1851 Census of Religion had indicated that more than half the population of England and Wales had worshipped somewhere on the last Sunday in March.[1] Added to this the great missionary societies continued to expand their spheres of work as the British Empire extended across the globe. Indeed, such was the mood that some churchmen began to speak and write in almost millennial terms, believing the great missionary movement might usher in the thousand year period of bliss 'when the earth would be filled with the glory of God as the waters cover the sea'. Below the surface, however, the mood was not quite so optimistic. Discoveries in science were beginning to challenge the traditional view of the world origins and the status of human beings. In 1859 Charles Darwin (1801–82) published *On the Origin of Species*, in which he maintained that species of living beings evolve by natural selection with the individuals best adapted to their circumstances surviving. Darwin's theory of evolution posed a direct challenge to the idea of special acts of creation. It also threatened the status of the human race which, he suggested in his later volume *The Descent of Man* (1871), had evolved from a species akin to the ape or monkey genera. Darwin's evolutionary theory was based on the notion that the fittest survive, and many sensitive individuals began to question whether a loving God could really have devised a creation which was based on suffering and bloodshed. Indeed the poet Tennyson wrote in his poem *In Memoriam*, published in 1850, of 'nature, red in tooth and claw'.

At the same time newly emerging techniques of higher criticism emanating from Germany were also posing serious questions about the inspiration and nature of the biblical material and in particular about the historicity of the New Testament Gospels. The substance of their theorizing was that the biblical documents were overlaid with mythical material and that this, coupled with successive re-writings and editings, had totally obscured their historical value. The problem, as they perceived it, was an impossible one of separating fact from fiction. There were doubts about the historicity of some of the events of Jesus's life and ministry. All this led scholars to a more critical view of the biblical literature and its interpretation. The various books had to be assessed in terms of their genre, which might be saga, law, wisdom, prophecy or poetry.

Alongside these challenges to biblical authority in the 1850s and 1860s, a number of High Churchmen were presenting another challenge to stability of the Church of England by introducing medieval and Roman Catholic ritual and practices into Anglican worship. This seemed to many bishops and clergy, Wigram among them, to be threatening the very Protestant Reformation basis on which the Church of England had been founded.

All his ministerial life Wigram had held strong Protestant evangelical convictions. He not only consented to the *Articles of Religion* and the authority of the Bible, they were both integral to his personal Christian faith. Despite his huge ministerial and pastoral commitments these were not issues from which Wigram could stand aside. Indeed, he felt compelled to contend with them both in the public arena in his triennial Visitation Charges, conferences with his clergy and in letters to the press.

ESSAYS AND REVIEWS AND BIBLICAL AUTHORITY

The growing doubts about the nature and authority of the Bible all somehow came together and found expression in the very year of Wigram's consecration as Bishop of Rochester with publication of a collection of articles entitled *Essays and Reviews*.[2] There were seven

Doubt, Ritualism and Bishop Colenso

contributors to this publication. Frederick Temple (1821–1902), was Headmaster of Rugby and later Archbishop of Canterbury. Rowland Williams (1817–70), was Professor of Hebrew and Vice-Principal of St David's College, Lampeter, who also held the small Wiltshire living of Broadchalke. Reputed to be occasionally hot-headed, he had a high reputation as a classical scholar, orientalist and theologian. Baden Powell (1796–1860) was Professor of Geometry at the University of Oxford, while Henry Bristow Wilson (1803–88), who edited the volume, was one of the tutors who condemned Tract 90 in 1841. He was vicar of Great Stoughton in Huntingdonshire. Charles Goodwin (1817–78), a Cambridge scholar and Egyptologist, was the only contributor not to be ordained. Mark Pattison (1813–84) was tutor at Lincoln College, and Benjamin Jowett (1817–93), later to be Master of Balliol College, was Professor of Greek in the University.

In a lengthy chapter entitled 'A Time of Preparation 1845–1858' in his study of *Essays and Reviews*, Ian Ellis pinpointed the year 1845 as a crucially important moment. It was in that year that John Henry Newman declared that he had been driven out from the University by the liberals. According to Ellis, the date 13 February 1845 was 'the birthday of modern liberalism in Oxford'. Ellis showed that the seven scholars who contributed to *Essays and Reviews* had been working and interacting with one another over a period of fifteen years.[3] The idea for the volume came from Wilson, who put the matter to Jowett, then rapidly becoming to be regarded as the leader of the liberal Christian circle at Oxford.[4] He welcomed the idea and explained the project to Arthur Stanley, a future Dean of Westminster, in the following terms.

> The object is to say we think freely within the limits of the Church of England. A notice will be prefixed that no one is responsible for any notions but his own. It is, however, an essential part of the plan that names shall be given... We do not wish to do anything rash or irritating to the public or the University, but we are determined not to submit to the abominable system of terrorism which prevents facts and makes true theological education impossible.[5]

The contributions which were made were varied, some of them being more offensive to traditional Christian views than others. Temple wrote on 'The Education of the World'. He pleaded for the fearless open-minded study of the Bible regardless of the consequences to orthodox belief, as the following passage from near the end of his essay makes plain.

> If geology proves to us that we must not interpret the first chapters of Genesis literally; if historical investigations shall show us that inspiration ... was not empowered to protect the narrative of the inspired writers from occasional inaccuracy; if careful criticism shall prove that there have been occasionally interpolations and forgeries in that Book, as in many others; the results should still be welcome.[6]

Rowland Williams in his contribution, entitled 'Bunsen's Biblical Researches',[7] wrote approvingly of many of the *avant-garde* views of the German scholar-diplomat, Baron Chevalier Bunsen, and sided with Bunsen's assertions that the Pentateuch was a compilation of 'gradual growth'; that Isaiah 40–56 was not written by Isaiah of Jerusalem but much later; that the Book of Daniel was not authentic history and belonged to the second century BC; that the servant in Isaiah 53 did not refer to Christ but was in all probability Jeremiah or possibly Baruch; and that the Epistle to the Hebrews was not written by Paul. These conclusions led Williams to state at one point: 'The Bible is, before all things, the written voice of the congregation' and again: 'The sacred writers acknowledge themselves men of like passions with ourselves'.

Baden Powell wrote 'On the Study of the Evidences of Christianity'. He was wary of endorsing the biblical miracles as such on the ground that divine interventions militated against the orderliness of nature.[8] 'It is thus', he wrote, 'the prevalent conviction that present day miracles are not to be expected, and consequently alleged marvels are commonly discredited.'[9] Henry Wilson wrote on 'The National Church', giving his own views as to the purpose of the National Church. He contended for a Church with a far less dogmatic basis, capable of embracing much wider sections of the nation. Wilson's views on inspiration were particularly offensive to orthodox Christians. He asserted that the biblical books were not 'miraculously inspired'.[10] And to term them the 'Word of God', a phrase 'never applied to them by any of the Scriptural authors', 'begs many a question', and, moreover, is a phrase which, 'according to Protestant principles, could never be applied to them by any sufficient authority from without'.[11]

Charles Goodwin wrote on 'The Mosaic Cosmogony'. In his essay he argued that a literal interpretation of the Genesis account of the Creation was at variance with the truths discovered by geologists. He maintained that the creation stories of Genesis were nothing but myths created by the Hebrews. In the final paragraph of his essay Goodwin concluded of Genesis: 'No one contends that it can be used as a basis of astronomical or geological teaching'.[12]

Mark Pattison wrote on 'Tendencies of Religious Thought in England, 1688–1750'. His essay was unpolemical and his role was as an historian of ideas. One of the themes of his discourse was the way in which the eighteenth century had begun to make use of common reason. Theologians of the nineteenth century must, he asserted, go on to use this reason as the judge of revelation.[13]

Benjamin Jowett wrote 'On the Interpretation of Scripture'. He was familiar with contemporary German biblical criticism and saw how much it had to teach the English students, hitherto insulated from such influences, 'by the blind veneration in which, in this country, the very letter of Scripture was usually held'. But in the matter of understanding Scripture, Jowett asserted that it must be treated 'like any other book'. 'The first step', he claimed, 'is to know the meaning', and again, 'No other science of hermeneutics is possible but an inductive one.' Jowett spelt out the matter in further detail:

> Scripture has one meaning—the meaning which it had to the mind of the prophet or evangelist who first uttered it . . . We have no reason to attribute to the prophet or evangelist any second or hidden sense different from that which appears on the surface.

Because Scripture is 'like any other book', attention must be paid to personal, local, historical and linguistic points of character. This can only be done 'in the same careful and impartial way that we ascertain the meaning of Sophocles and Plato'.[14]

Joseph Cotton Wigram

REACTION TO THE *ESSAYS*

Reaction to the *Essays* was widespread and for the most part unequivocally critical and condemnatory. By and large the Protestant Nonconformists remained somewhat aloof and the main Congregationalist and Methodist scholarly journals made little or no comment. In contrast, however, the Baptists and Baptist Union were forthright in their opposition. *The Freeman*, the Baptist Union's denominational newspaper, began an article on the *Essays* by stating that 'justice, love and truth compel us to condemn this book'.[15] At the same time the writer was impressed that 'as a controversial book the volume is nowhere disfigured by bitterness or scorn' and each writer seems 'imbued with a gentle spirit'. After noting Rowland Williams's unreserved praise for Bunsen's biblical researches, the volume's contention that the Red Sea 'may be interpreted with the latitude of poetry' and that the fifty-third chapter of Isaiah contains 'no reference to Christ at all', *The Freeman*'s reviewer commented on the essayists as follows.

> The ultimate issue to which they would lead us is very clear, viz., a rejection of all that the Word of God contains, which we may happen to deem irreconcilable with the dictates of our reason. From henceforth, Scripture contains no mysteries ... all God's thoughts absolutely come within the compass of our own.[16]

The evangelical publication, *The Christian Observer*, printed an article on the *Essays* in June 1860 entitled 'Broad Church Theology', in which it dubbed Rowland Williams the 'most dangerous of the essayists, whose contribution amounted to forty-three pages of reckless infidelity'.[17] The same paper cynically concluded, 'The present volume is meant to establish the principle that a man may retain the orders and benefices of the Church without believing the Bible'. In short, it continued, 'the volume is the Tract No. XC of the Broad Church'. The other main evangelical paper, *The Record*, sounded the same note of alarm and denounced the seven essayists as 'septem contra Christum'.[18]

Wigram clearly endorsed the views expressed by both *The Christian Observer* and *The Record*, though it was not until 1863, when the book had been more widely read, that he began to publicly challenge its contents and writers. Towards the end of 1863 he organised a series of lectures in various parts of his diocese on biblical authority. The lecturer, the Revd Dr Joseph Baylee, the Principal of St Aidan's College, Birkenhead, was commended by Wigram in his introduction for 'carrying on a great work in training young men'. Wigram praised Baylee for his 'valuable lecture' and publicised the fact the similar meetings had been held at Rochester, Gravesend and Waltham Abbey.[19] A week later Wigram issued a circular to all the rural deans of the diocese suggesting that they should take a stand against 'the sceptical objections and perverse criticism put forth of late'.[20] They could do this by encouraging clergy within their deaneries 'to instruct the people concerning the authenticity and inspiration of Holy Scripture'. He also reminded them that 'many of our Nonconformist brethren look to us as standard bearers in times of special emergency'. Such courses could be held in Lent with clergy perhaps sharing lectures with a neighbouring parish. These lectures, Wigram urged, 'would prove 'the wonderful effects of the word of God on the hearts of men in all ages' and 'its adaption to the wants of fallen and corrupted beings'.[21] They would also explain 'the nature of the atonement of Christ' and enable hearers 'to give a reason for the hope that is in them'.[22] Wigram concluded his circular with the shrewd observation that 'the danger of the Church does not arise from having her doctrines attacked, or her privileges assailed, but from her ministers being unfaithful or her people being unholy'.[23]

Wigram revisited the issue again in his second triennial Visitation in the autumn of 1864. He devoted a substantial section to the dangers he perceived in *Essays and Reviews*, which he considered to be a particular hindrance to the work in the diocese.[24] Wigram began as follows:

> A topic in some respects more painful is reserved for my concluding remarks. I refer to the fresh outbreak of old scepticism, and more than tacit resistance to the authority of the Word of God. Some brethren in the ministry have forsaken us, and others remain with us who do not acknowledge God's truth as held by the church. The dissemination of writings by men of repute in opposition to the old doctrines expounded by such men as Pearson, Hooker, and Waterland, and the spread of such opinions by the periodical press, cannot fail to injure those who are unstable in the faith.[25]

He went on to say that the major purpose of his Charge was not to spend time refuting the errors of the essayists, as 'these gainsayers have been met in their most devious paths, and resisted effectually by men of at least equal power and learning with themselves'.[26] Indeed, he pointed out, that 'rarely in any past period of opposition to the faith have so many sound and able treatises issued from the press to meet an emergency of the same kind'. He also took great encouragement from the fact that the book had been formally condemned by Convocation and that the church as a whole had not been evilly affected 'by the monstrous and strange opposition to her doctrines'.[27] His concern was that members of the congregations in the diocese would be led astray. Indeed, *Essays and Reviews* had already had a 'pernicious effect' in the district of Rochester. He took no encouragement from the fact that the writings of the essayists had never been seen or were unknown in many a town or village. However, the fact was their influence would find an echo through the 'low press in the public house and the beer shop, or places of common resort throughout the land'.[28] Wigram warned his clergy of the dangers of indifference and worldliness, which he regarded as 'unbelief' and 'the fruits of our evil heart'.[29] We must not, he asserted, be fearful of introducing controversy when we know the truth is at stake.

Against this major and significant issue Wigram had stood strong on his conservative evangelical convictions. Along with the other of bishops appointed by Palmerston[30] he was doubtless gratified that the *Essays* were condemned in the Lower House of Convocation by 39 votes to 19 and in the Upper House by 8 votes to 2.[31]

BISHOP COLENSO

When it came to churchmen with liberal or revisionist tendencies (such as the essayists) undermining biblical authority, Wigram's *bête noire* was John William Colenso (1814–83), the Bishop of Natal. In his earlier years Colenso had been a Fellow of St John's College, Cambridge, and had followed this with a spell in a Norfolk country living. Whilst at Cambridge he was much influenced by Frederick Denison Maurice's universalism. As a result, when he was consecrated bishop and went out to Africa in 1853, he felt it unnecessary to convert the indigenous peoples he encountered there, but merely taught them. Soon after his arrival Colenso set about the task of translating the Old and New Testaments into Zulu. He was much perturbed when his Zulu assistant expressed his revulsion at the brutal command in ancient Hebrew law in Exodus 2: 20–1, which allowed that a man might beat his male or female slave provided they did not die in consequence. The experience challenged Colenso to re-think a whole range of issues, including the Creation and the Flood stories. In 1861 he created a stir by questioning the doctrine of eternal punishment in his *Commentary on the Epistle to the Romans*. This, however, was nothing compared to the positive uproar which resulted when the first part of *The Pentateuch and the Book of Joshua Critically Examined* was published late in October 1862. In this volume Colenso occupied himself with the minutiae of Old Testament detail, such as the great ages of the heroes of the patriarchal era, and logistical problems associated with the temple rituals and the wilderness wanderings. In one chapter based on Joshua 8: 34–5, he considered how Moses could have read all the Book of the Law before all the congregation of Israel, a company which the Revd T. Scott had calculated on the basis of Exodus 12 to be 'not much less than two millions'.[32] 'Surely', Colenso commented, 'no human voice, unless strengthened by a miracle of which the Scripture tells us nothing, could have reached the ears of a crowded mass of people, as large as the population of London.'[33] In another section, he considered the size of the Court of the Tabernacle in relation to the size of 'the whole congregation of Israel', who were, according to Numbers 10: 3–4, ordered together at the door of the Tabernacle. Colenso assumed that they must have stood in consecutive lines not just in front of the door but the width of the courtyard, in which case they stretched away 'for a distance of more than 100,000 feet,—in fact nearly *twenty miles!*'[34] 'It is inconceivable' he wrote, 'how under such circumstances "all the Assembly", "the whole Congregation" could have been summoned to attend "at the door of the Tabernacle" by express command of Almighty God.'[35] In another discussion related to the Tabernacle, Colenso considered the sacrificial duties of the priests, of whom there were only three—Aaron and his sons, Eleazar and Ithamar. Just attending to the childbirth offerings of pigeons for approximately

250 births a day each priest would have had to eat daily '88 for his own portion, "in the most holy place".[36] Colenso concluded with a scornful dismissal of the Pentateuch by stating that the 'narrative, whatever may be its value and meaning, cannot be regarded as historically true'.[37] For his painstaking research, Colenso's metropolitan, Bishop Gray of Cape Town, a Tractarian conservative, deposed him in 1863.[38] Colenso, however, appealed to the Judicial Committee of the Privy Seal, which reversed the sentence in his favour in 1865. The controversy eventually dragged on even after his death and the schism in the South African church has never been healed.

Colenso's writing were deeply offensive to the mid-Victorian public and there were a number of public rebuttals in the Christian press and published sermons. The bench of bishops met together on several occasions in January and February 1863 to discuss Colenso's writings. On 9 February Archibald Tait drafted an address on behalf of the episcopal bench to Colenso, who was then in England, urging him to 'earnest prayer and deeper study of God's Word', that he might 'under the guidance of the Holy Spirit, be restored to a state of belief in which you may be able with a clear conscience again discharge the duties of our sacred office.'[39] In a later speech in Convocation, which Wigram would have undoubtedly endorsed, Tait said that he had not the slightest doubt that Bishop Colenso 'had published most dangerous books—books of the tendency of which I doubt whether he was aware when he published them'. 'Colenso', he continued, 'has already done sufficient to convince us [the bench of bishops] that he is quite unfit to exercise the office of a bishop in the Church of England.'[40]

In December 1862 Wigram penned a letter to Colenso on account of his radical views in which, in the words of *The Essex Standard*, 'he impugns the authenticity of the Pentateuch'. The paper printed the letter in full.

> My dear Bishop of Natal,—I am led to address you with real sorrow, and under a painful sense of duty, to make a request that you will not, under any circumstances, be induced to take part in the religious services of the Church within the limits of my diocese. I have read and carefully considered your recent publication, with intense regret that you have been so grievously misled from

the truths which you professed to hold at your ordination and subsequent consecration; and I see no other course to be pursued for the protection of the congregations and parishes intrusted to my care than to submit this remonstrance against your officiating in any church of my diocese. Neither the intimation given in the preface of your book, p. 27, that you cannot comply with invitations to preach, &c., nor the confidence which I feel that no clergyman with whom I am officially connected, who had read your book, would invite you to minister in his parish, supersedes the necessity I feel for this letter. In no other manner can I divest myself of the responsibility I should incur, if I heard of your officiating in these parts, than by knowledge that I had emphatically protested against your doing so. I ought to add that it will not be possible to avoid some measure of publicity attending this communication, because it will be my duty to send a copy of it to my Archdeacons for the information of the clergy. I remain, &c.

J. C. ROCHESTER.
Danbury Palace, Chelmsford, December 9.[41]

The Christian World commended Wigram's published letter as 'a model of politeness and firmness in happy union'. It will have done more, the paper asserted, to persuade Dr Colenso to re-examine his position, in relation to the Bible, than the most vehement denunciations of heresies.[42]

Wigram's letter showed him to be a wise pastor and guide to his clergy. On the one hand he was firm in his conviction that Colenso was undermining the basis of the Christian faith without solid evidence and on the other he had faith in his clergy that they would comply with his request. In fact, many of them had written letters in support of the action he had taken.

In the third week of January 1863 *The Chelmsford Chronicle* printed the reply which Wigram had written to the clergy in seven of his rural deaneries, who had 'presented addresses expressing sympathy with, and gratitude for' his stance against Bishop Colenso.[43] In his reply Wigram stated that he felt constrained to offer a few remarks for those who have neither learning nor the opportunity of obtaining of the book. His first point was that Colenso had freely acknowledged that the views he had expressed were of 'a comparatively recent date'.[44] Second, the Bishop of Natal had stated that though the views expressed were new to him they were not new to many of his English readers. Wigram countered that if he had taken the trouble to scrutinise the relevant literature he would have discovered his doubts concerning 'the phenomena of the Pentateuch' had already been answered by Leslie, Chandler, Leland and others.[45] His third point was that Colenso's 'unacquaintance with the Hebrew language' led him to repeat the mistranslations of the Authorised Version.

In the middle section of his letter Wigram drew attention to some criticisms that had been raised against Colenso by Dr McCaul of King's College, London. He did not accept 'the plain testimony of our Lord Jesus Christ himself to the truth of the Holy Scriptures as they existed when he was on Earth'.[46] He objects to the Lord's testimony to Moses and thinks that the Lord was simply speaking 'the current popular language of the day'. McCaul cited several examples of Colenso's sceptical views. He asserted that 'it cannot seriously be maintained that as a young child Jesus possessed a knowledge surpassing that of the most pious adults of his nation'.[47] He distinctly repudiated what we term the authority of the of God's word stating, 'how hollow is the ground upon which we have so long been standing' with reference to the inspiration of Scripture.[48]

Wigram concluded his response to the deaneries on a more personal note referring in particular to the Bishop of Natal's haughty attitude in predicting 'that I shall adopt such opinions as he holds, and revoke the inhibition I have put forth'.[49] To this Wigram was adamant that everything he had heard about Colenso's opinions led him to a contrary conclusion and deep regret that he had so grievously erred from the faith he had solemnly pledged himself to hold and inculcate at his ordination and consecration. He entreated the clergy of the diocese of Rochester 'to offer up prayer fervently to God on his behalf, that the Holy Spirit would indeed bring him to the acknowledgment of God's truth'.[50]

Wigram still had strong words for Bishop Colenso when he gave his second Charge to the clergy of the diocese in Rochester Cathedral on the 21 October 1864.[51] He observed that 'Great perplexity had also arisen as to the mode of restraining the colonial bishop who has erred most grievously in the exercise of his office, by which he has excited such strong reprobation among ourselves, and such determined measures of opposition in the South African Church'.[52] Wigram expressed his satisfaction that nothing had occurred to suggest the faith of the church has been in the least disturbed. He was also encouraged to have received almost unanimous support from clergy over the prohibition he had issued against Dr Colenso being allowed to officiate anywhere in the diocese.[53]

RITUALISM

The English Church in medieval times had, of course, been part of the Western Catholic Church. In that era before the Reformation its worship had been characterised by a good deal of ritual centred on the Mass and the sacramental system. In addition, there were many monastic houses with their daily rounds of processional services and sung offices which contributed to the development of ceremonial. Much of this heritage was eradicated by the sixteenth-century Protestant reformers in their desire to recover a simpler way of religious life and worship that was more in keeping with the New Testament and early church practices. For the most part English church worship remained plain and unadorned until the middle years of the nineteenth century, when a series of events combined to create a renewed desire to recover medieval ritual in the Church of England.

The main impetus to this change came from the second generation of the Oxford Movement. Its initial phase is generally held to have extended from 1833 to 1841 and was so called because its leaders were fellows and tutors of the University. In early days it was often also referred to as 'Tractarianism' on account of the publication of their views in a series of 'Tracts for the Times'. It was almost exclusively focused on doctrinal issues and, most importantly, the nature of the church. The issue which began to trouble churchmen in the mid-Victorian years was the fact that the Church of England was beginning to lose its influence as the national church. Members of Parliament were no longer required to be committed Anglicans and this meant that those of other faiths, or even none, were able to have a say in the government of the established church. The Oxford Movement felt that this state of affairs was entirely wrong and that the church as the body of Christ must assert its authority over an increasingly secular nation. In their endeavour to achieve this John Henry Newman and others began to argue that the Church of England was part of the one Holy Catholic Church and could trace a direct spiritual and binding link all the way back to St Peter and the Apostolic Church of the first century. This was brought about because the spirit which the apostles had received from Jesus was then passed down by the laying-on of hands, first by the apostles to those they appointed, and then on by the bishops they appointed and so on down through the generations and centuries to the present time. From this tradition the Tractarians asserted that the Church of England was an integral part of the body of Christ and its priestly ministry had a unique apostolic status being a part of the One Holy, Catholic and Apostolic Church.

This then led the Oxford leaders to focus their attentions on the first four Christian centuries, when the Catholic Church could be said to be undivided, at least in a public sense, and therefore construed as Catholic or universal. As they researched and studied the church in this period, they re-discovered a number of beliefs and practices which had featured in the late-medieval church, albeit in a more extreme form. In particular, it became clear to them that churches in both the East and West of the Roman empire believed Christ to be uniquely present in or through the consecrated Eucharistic bread and wine. Early communion liturgies expressed the view that after the priest had consecrated the bread and wine they were either changed in status or in nature or in both status and nature. It was also apparent that on occasions some of the Eucharistic elements were kept back at the end of the service to be taken to the sick and those who were too far away to join the main church gathering. The Eucharist was also beginning to be understood as a sacrifice or something to be offered to God.

In their study of the undivided church of the first four centuries the second generation Tractarians also encountered other aspects of church life and worship which no longer featured in the liturgies of the *Book of Common Prayer*. These included the high status accorded to the Virgin Mary, prayers for the faithful departed, fasting, and the practice of celibacy. Some of these, and other more recent Roman Catholic practice, they began to introduce into the Church of England. In this they were also encouraged by the 'Ornaments Rubric' at the front of the 1662 *Book of Common Prayer* which explicitly stated that 'such ornaments of the Church, and the Ministers thereof, at all times of their ministration, shall be retained and be in use, as were in this Church of England, by authority of parliament, in the second year of the reign of King Edward VI'. By this means they were able to maintain that they were simply adhering to the original regulations and that it was perfectly legal for the priest to wear 'a white alb plain with vestment or cope' and to celebrate Communion not at the north side of the table but 'afore the altar' as specified before the Prayer of Consecration. In a number of churches in London and elsewhere other Romish ritualistic practices began to feature in Tractarian churches, including the use of incense and candles on altars and Communion tables, reservation of the sacrament, benediction and auricular confession. Robed choirs and processional services started to become fashionable.

Wigram along with all the almost all the bench of bishops was deeply perturbed by these developments. As they saw it the re-introduction of medieval practice and ritual was a denial of the Reformation basis on which the Church of England had been founded in the sixteenth century. For Wigram and his fellow bishops the authority on which the Church of England was based was not the undivided church of the fourth century but the apostolic teaching and practice as recorded in the apostolic writings of the New Testament. As far as they were concerned Article 6 said it all.

> Holy Scripture containeth all things necessary to salvation: so that whatsoever is not read therein, nor may be proved thereby, is not to be required by any man, that it should be believed as an article of the Faith, or be thought requisite or necessary to salvation. In the name of Holy Scripture we do understand those canonical Books of the Old and New Testament, of whose authority was never in any doubt in the Church.[54]

In his first Visitation Wigram had expressed great concern at the emergence of ritualism within his diocese. He began gently referring to 'brethren of active and earnest minds' who concerned themselves with the external adornments of religion but soon got down to the basics.

> The sanctuary is, with them, honoured with costly decorations, the worship elevated by peculiar tones of voice. They are fond of reverting to the ancient ecclesiastical rites, and of reintroducing the vestments, and manners, of times gone by. Symbolic representations are used to impress the senses, and by certain conventional gestures and attitudes they seek to influence their people, and lead them, as they imagine through these externals, to adore more fitly the Great Unseen. It is not enough with them that architectural beauties, and decent attire of our sacred edifices should be restored, but they must needs embody doctrines in decorations, and hazard the revival of practices which belong to the corrupt Romish system out of which our nation was mercifully brought at the Reformation.[55]

Wigram, like many other Protestant-minded members of the Established Church, was still reeling from the restoration of the Roman Catholic hierarchy and dioceses in Britain in 1850 and Pope Pius IX's appointment of Cardinal Nicholas Wiseman as the first Archbishop of Westminster. The fact that clergy in his own diocese were actually mimicking Roman rites and traditions was the ultimate in disloyalty and would only serve to alienate people from their parish churches and drive them to join the Nonconformists. Wigram went on to argue that ritualism was unsuited to the needs of the time and inconsistent with the simplicity of the Christian faith. He followed this straight talking by expressing his satisfaction 'that the great majority of the 820 pastors and 649 folds whom I am meeting in this Visitation would utter one unanimous disclaimer of the opinions and practices which I have unhesitatingly condemned as a contradiction to the Christian ministry'.[56]

For Wigram, the battle with ritualism was soon to impact on him in a more personal way. In the following year, 1861, Nathaniel Woodard of Woodard Schools' fame organised a great meeting at the Sheldonian Theatre in Oxford to promote his scheme for providing boarding schools for the lower middle classes. The University's Vice-Chancellor, Francis Jeune (1806–68), agreed to chair the meeting and Wigram consented to second the main speech, which was made by W. E. Gladstone. As they made their way into the Theatre Wigram was shocked that the invited company were presented with an anonymous handbill, written, as it turned out, by Charles Golightly, denouncing Woodard's scheme as disguised popery. Jeune treated them with indifference and felt that the meeting had been a great success.

However, during the weeks that followed both Wigram and Jeune received reports that suggested that the situation was not exactly how they had perceived it. Indeed, friends had expressed concern that he might appear to be endorsing illegal ritualistic practice. Eventually, on 23 January 1862, Wigram wrote to Jeune stating that he had received a communication informing him that St Nicholas College, Shoreham, where Woodard was Provost, was encouraging practices 'most incongruous with the teaching of the reformed church' and that 'particular confession' was being strongly advocated.[57] 'Under such circumstances', Wigram opined, 'the part that I was led to take in your university is easily open to misrepresentation, and has been greatly misunderstood; and I am desirous to put myself right with the public and my friends.' Wigram concluded by asking Jeune if he was still satisfied in respect of the Woodard Institutions or whether he had reason to change his mind',[58] and he was doubtless pleased to receive Jeune's unexpectedly prompt reply only two days later. 'Concurring in your lordship's views generally', Jeune wrote, he felt he 'must now suspend, and shall feel obliged, though with regret, wholly to withdraw my support of the excellent scheme of Mr. Woodard, unless, after a free and searching inquiry, it can be made evident that our distrust is without foundation.'[59] Wigram's correspondence with Jeune, together with the many letters he had received from friends, drew him into the heart of the controversy. Consequently he began ensuring that his views were made known to number of prominent individuals including 'the Vice-Chancellor of Cambridge, the Master of Trinity (my old private tutor), the Master of Jesus and through him the Bishop of Ely and I have spoken to the Bishop of Norwich'.[60]

One of those with whom Wigram inevitably corresponded was Charles Pourtales Golightly (1807–85). It was, after all, his pamphlet warning against the dangers of the Woodard school practices, that Wigram had received on going into the meeting at the Sheldonian Theatre. Educated at Eton and Oriel College, Golightly had come from a wealthy Huguenot family. For a time he was curate to Archibald Campbell Tait at Baldon and later held the position of Afternoon Lecturer at St Andrew's Church, Headington. Although wealthy, living in Oxford and often waited on by a footman, Golightly had great compassion for the poor. His early and strong opposition to the views of Newman and the Tractarians[61] led him to become a life-long opponent of Romanism and ritualism. In 1858 he had launched a blistering attack on the practices of Cuddesdon College. R. W. Greaves has written of Golightly 'that from his youth he was set in a rigidly conservative mould' and he 'continued with unremitting zeal, for well-nigh another forty years, in his campaigns to save the Church of England from the dangers and novelties, Tractarian or Liberal'.[62]

On 1 January 1862 Wigram wrote to Golightly from Danbury Palace saying that he had read Golighty's letters and that he too was 'increasingly convinced of the necessity of making a strong stand against this insidious encroachment on our reformed principles'.[63] Two days later Wigram followed up with another letter enclosing some of the supporting correspondence he had received, including testimony about one of Robert Liddell's curates at St Barnabas, Pimlico,[64] who had left his position on account of the church's ritualism. Wigram urged Golightly 'to restrain your use of the papers' and return them as soon as you can because the Bishop of Oxford had asked to read them.[65]

Wigram's correspondence with Jeune was published as a pamphlet, almost certainly in early February 1862.[66] One consequence was that The English Church Union then waded into the battle against Wigram. On 10 March 1862 they produced a memorial, in which they expressed 'much surprise' at having read a letter signed by Wigram 'in which your lordship withdraws your sanction from certain institutions for the education of the middle classes on the ground that "extensive inquiries" have given you the strongest distrust of the principles on which the institutions are administered'. The memorialists then offered a defence of the Woodard schools' practice of 'particular confession', confession and fasting, arguing that they were all in accordance with the rules of the church.

One week later, on 17 March, Wigram replied from Danbury Palace to the Union's President, Colin Lindsay.[67] Regarding 'particular confession', Wigram pointed out that the Church of England only permitted it in the case of 'certain adult members who are in a grievous state of mind'. The rubric also leaves such individuals free to go to any ministers of the church whereas pupils at St Nicholas College are confined with the walls of the institution and may only go to the school Chaplain-Confessor. Wigram was clear that our church does not allow confession 'to be pressed upon the minds of children who are placed under the school's absolute control'. He was also quite sure 'that our church does not, like that institution, arrange any distinction of food to be observed by her members'. Wigram shrewdly ended his reply by noting that the ECU had published some of his and Jeune's views, which they felt 'may cause much disturbance of mind to certain religious persons'. He therefore presumed they would have no objection to his making public the contents of their Memorial. He graciously asked the favour of a reply on this last point.

Lindsay was not, however, prepared to leave the matter and replied to Wigram on behalf of the ECU on 24 March 1862. Noting that Wigram did allow confession on the part of adults 'in the case of certain grievous situations', he went on to point out that 'one rule of the school is that express permission must be given by parents in cases of confession'. He concluded by stating that where differences of opinion exist as to the carrying out of fasting, confession and other matters enjoined in the formularies the church, the bishop of the diocese should make the decision.[68]

Wigram wrote back on 1 April saying he did not find any strength in the arguments Lindsay had set out, and, he concluded, 'I am still strongly of the opinion that it is most injurious to the young to be subjected to compulsory food restrictions and that the confession on the part of young children should be encouraged'.[69] He was doubtless heartened when on the following day he received a Memorial from Edward Harper, President of The Central Protestant Institute, denouncing the 'odious, polluting, and abominable confessional', 'bread worship', 'prayers for the dead', and other 'popish designs' of Tractarianism.[70]

However, by this time Wigram had reached the conclusion that the time had come for him to withdraw from the front line of the battle. He had already written to Golightly on 18 January 1862 'With regard

Joseph Cotton Wigram

to Mr Woodard's institutions, I really see nothing that I can do. The Matter shall have my deepest consideration, but it seems to me, the Bp of Chichester has taken the whole burden upon himself, and the Oxford inquirers declare he has done so'. As to his personal feelings Wigram wrote, 'It is very, very sad' and 'I will think much about the matter, which perplexes me sorely, as to the proper course of duty'.[71] The letters at Lambeth Palace Library contain one last short note from Wigram urging Golightly to continue the battle by supplying Jeune with material.[72] While Wigram withdrew to the side lines he doubtless found comfort in Golightly's forthright determination to pursue the enemy. Indeed, Golightly continued to fight to the end of his days. Always on the look-out for incipient Romanism he carried on a massive correspondence warning friends, acquaintances and even strangers of the latest Tractarian innovations. Among those to whom he wrote were Edward Bickersteth, Bishop O'Brien, Charles Bird, Archdeacon J. H. Browne, George S. Faber, Charles A. Heurtley, William Goode and prominent churchmen such as Bishop Blomfield and Samuel Wilberforce. He sent letters to the church and to national and local newspapers, usually signed 'a Master of Arts' of Oxford.[73]

Notes

1. See for example Thompson (ed.) 1972, pp. 147–55; Chadwick 1970, part 2, pp. 225–33.
2. See Wilson (ed.) 1860.
3. Ellis 1960, p. 12.
4. *Ibid.*, p. 30.
5. Vidler 1961, p. 124.
6. F. Temple, 'The Education of the World', in Wilson (ed.) 1860, p. 47
7. R. Williams, 'Bunsen's Biblical Researches', in Wilson (ed.) 1860, pp. 50–93.
8. B. Powell, 'On the Study of the Evidences of Christianity', in Wilson (ed.) 1860, pp. 94–144.
9. *Ibid.*, p. 107.
10. H. B. Wilson, 'Séances historiques de Genève: The National Church', in Wilson (ed.) 1860, pp. 145–206.
11. *Ibid.*, p. 175.
12. C. Goodwin, 'The Mosaic Cosmogony', in Wilson (ed.) 1860, pp. 207–53.

13 M. Pattison, 'Tendencies of Religious Thought in England, 1688–1750', in Wilson (ed.) 1860, pp. 254–329.
14 B. Jowett, 'On the Interpretation of Scripture', in Wilson (ed.) 1860, pp. 330–443.
15 *The Freeman*, 27 June 1860.
16 Ibid.
17 *The Christian Observer*, June 1860.
18 *The Record*, cited in Reardon 1971, p. 340.
19 *The Chelmsford Chronicle*, 11 December 1863.
20 *The Essex Standard*, 16 December 1863.
21 Ibid.
22 Ibid.
23 Ibid.
24 J. C. Wigram, *A Charge ... 1864*, p. 50.
25 *The Western-super-Mare Gazette*, 29 October 1864.
26 Ibid.
27 Ibid.
28 Ibid.
29 Ibid.
30 See Scotland 2000, pp. 88–9.
31 *Chronicle of Convocation*, pp. 1683 and 1830, cited in Davidson and Benham 1891, vol. 1, p. 322.
32 Colenso 1862, p. 36.
33 Ibid., p. 37.
34 Ibid., p. 33.
35 Ibid., p. 34.
36 Ibid., p. 35.
37 Ibid., p. 128
38 Hinchliff 1964, p. 115.
39 Davidson and Benham 1891, vol. 1, pp. 342–3.
40 Ibid., vol. 1, p. 361.
41 *The Essex Standard*, 24 December 1862.
42 Quoted in *The Essex Herald*, 6 January 1863.
43 *The Chelmsford Chronicle*, 16 January 1863.
44 Ibid.
45 Ibid.
46 Ibid.
47 Ibid.
48 Ibid.
49 Ibid.
50 Ibid.

Joseph Cotton Wigram

51   *Western-super-Mare Gazette*, 29 October 1864.
52   *Ibid.*
53   *Ibid.*
54   Article 6 of the 39 Articles of Religion, see *The Book of Common Prayer*.
55   J. C. Wigram, *A Charge ... 1860*, p. 25.
56   *Ibid.*, p. 26.
57   *The Chelmsford Chronicle*, 18 April 1863. This edition of the *Chronicle* published an extended correspondence between Wigram and others on the issue of ritualism.
58   See *St Nicholas Middle Schools: A Correspondence between ... the Bishop of Rochester, and the ... Vice-Chancellor ...*, 1862.
59   F. Jeune, letter to the Bishop of Rochester, 25 January 1862, in *St Nicholas Middle Schools: A Correspondence*, 1862, and *The Chelmsford Chronicle*, 18 April 1862.
60   J. C. Wigram, letter to 'My dear Sir' (possibly Charles Golightly) regarding Vice-Chancellor Jeune and ritualism at St Nicholas College. LPL, MS 172g.
61   See Greaves 1958, pp. 209–28.
62   *Ibid.*, p. 228.
63   J. C. Wigram, letter to the Revd C. P. Golightly, 1 January 1862, LPL, MS 168.
64   For Liddell, see Cornish 1910, part 2, pp. 13–16 and 84.
65   J. C. Wigram, letter to the Revd C. P. Golightly, 3 January 1862, LPL, MS 170.
66   *St Nicholas College Middle Schools: A Correspondence between ... the Bishop of Rochester, and the ... Vice-Chancellor*, 1862. In a letter to an unidentified correspondent (possibly Charles Golightly), dated 25 January 1862, Wigram wrote of his expectation that Vice-Chancellor, would allow their correspondence about St Nicholas College to be published, LPL, MS 172.
67   J. C. Wigram, letter to C. Lindsay, 17 March 1862, in *The Chelmsford Chronicle*, 18 April 1862.
68   C. Lindsay, letter to the Bishop of Rochester, 24 March 1862, in *The Chelmsford Chronicle*, 18 April 1862.
69   *Ibid.*
70   *The Chelmsford Chronicle*, 18 April 1862.
71   J. C. Wigram, letter to Revd C. P. Golightly, 18 January 1862, LPL, MS 175.
72   J. C. Wigram, letter to Revd C. P. Golightly, 31 January 1862, LPL, MS 174.
73   Toon 1979, pp. 39–40, 53–6 and 83–5.

7

Pastor of the Clergy and People

The point in time at which Wigram began his episcopate was one in which almost every diocese in England had pockets of indigent poverty and squalor. In his previous role as Archdeacon of Winchester he had become deeply aware of the deprivation and disease suffered by the working poor in both Portsmouth and Southampton. In fact he quoted in one of his publications a passage from a pamphlet entitled *Sanitary Condition, &c., of the Borough of Portsmouth, including the Isle of Portsea* describing the filthy, insanitary and squalid conditions endured by many of the inhabitants (see pages 34–5).

He was doubtless fully aware that one of the reasons he had been elevated to the episcopal bench was his pastoral gifts. Indeed, Palmerston, who had appointed him, took the view that bishops are to the church what generals are to the army.[1] He regarded their chief duties as 'watching over the clergy of their diocese, seeing that they perform their parochial duties properly, and preserving harmony between the clergy and the laity'.[2] Carew St John Mildmay (1800–78), whom Wigram appointed Archdeacon of Essex in 1862, later highlighted the bishop's concern to mobilise the laity in the church's mission. 'From the first of his coming among them', Mildmay declared, 'he led the way in introducing what was acknowledged by all to be a great work, the bringing of the laity to occupy their proper place in the great work of Christ's church. They knew well how earnest he was on all occasions in flinging himself among the laity and asking their co-operation. He was emphatically the layman's bishop.'[3]

Joseph Cotton Wigram

THE CLERGY

During his time as Bishop of Rochester Wigram gave particular attention to the needs of his clergy and their lives and ministries. As has been already been noted this extended to the state of their clothing, houses, salaries and sporting activities, including cricket. He even added his particular disapproval of their growing beards. He was mindful of the dysfunctional behaviour which was linked with particular sports and pastimes. In August 1860 he signed a public document along with a number of his clergy and other town's people against the annual Chatham races which he maintained engendered a bad atmosphere. It led to *The Saturday Review* dubbing him as 'a bishop of little things'.[4]

Wigram was concerned that his clergy should do all in their power to preserve the Lord's Day as a time for rest and worship. In January 1863 *The Chelmsford Chronicle* printed the text of a memorial from the Archbishops, which all the bishops of the Church of England, including Wigram, had signed. It presented the directors of railway companies with five reasons 'to discontinue the running excursion trains on the Lord's-day'. It is, the document asserted, 'in accordance with the will of God, and essential to the well-being of man, that the Lord's-day be kept holy for the worship of God and the performance of religious duties'.[5] Wigram's forthright defence of the Sabbath day was a conviction shared by the Victorian evangelical world. He also expressed his concern that in many parishes the role of the Christian faith 'is rarely acknowledged' in the annual harvest celebrations'. Yet, he continued, the remedy would be easy at the harvest feast itself by an enlargement of the grace that is said followed by the Lord's Prayer, by the reading of a short passage of Scripture and a contribution from school singers.[6]

Wigram kept in touch with those clergy who were in need through the help and knowledge which he gleaned from of his rural deans. He also held frequent meetings in rural deaneries, where he advised clergy about the sermon topics, the conduct of the occasional offices, the needs of their parochial schools and he warned of the dangers of ritualism and liberal theology. We see his passionate concern over the latter issue in his letter to all clergy urging them not to allow or invite Bishop Colenso of Natal to preach or minister in their parishes. He also

Pastor of the Clergy and People

urged them to support and encourage home and overseas missions both as individuals and in their parishes.

Wigram was widely known for his warm, outgoing and welcoming nature.* In August 1861 *The Chelmsford Chronicle* reported that the group of inspectors he called to Danbury Palace to consider issues relating to National Schools had been 'sumptuously entertained' there.[7] Canon O. W. Davys, the rector of Wheathampstead in the Archdeaconry of Hertford, remembered Wigram fondly as 'kind and hospitable, but so thoroughly low church that he did not get on well with all of us'. He continued, 'No one can tell now what he would have thought of our present bearded Bishops, for he devoted some time in one of his charges in speaking against "this peculiarity in cultivating the hair;" but I was happily right with him on that point'.[8]

PREACHING

Wigram regarded preaching as a central concern of the ordained ministry. He was meticulous and conscientious in his sermon preparation. Accounts and summaries of his sermons in the local papers and in the few addresses that he published reveal a carefully chosen text and theme. They show evidence of good everyday illustrations and a straightforward structure with two or three clear points. In his days as Archdeacon and then as Bishop Wigram became increasingly concerned both about what was being preached and the manner in which it was being delivered. In April 1859 he noted; 'our own church rulers declare that our preaching in general is too little suited to attract the presence and gain the attention of a large portion of the flock'.[9] With this in mind he made the subject of his twelfth General Charge to the Archdeaconry of Winchester, 'How to Preach in our Ordinary Congregations'.[10] Ever the modest man, Wigram did not claim to be giving a worthy representation of good preaching to the English Church. Rather he offered his piece 'for the purpose of awakening in others earnest thoughts on this great work of the ministry'.[11]

---

* Bishop Charles Sumner found him 'somewhat cold in manner', perhaps because theirs was a rather more formal relationship.

Joseph Cotton Wigram

In this Charge Wigram sought to highlight 'What can be learned about preaching from our Lord and his followers'.[12] Throughout, his approach was practical and he gave helpful advice on how not to preach. Too many preachers, he noted, 'forget the power of the word of God' and 'put too much faith in human instrumentality'.[13] 'We must', he continued, 'beware of strong intonations of voice and gesture used to impress the hearers and produce interest and excitement.'[14] He urged 'constant application of the text' asking questions such as, 'Are you tempted by sensuality? This was Joseph's lot and he withstood. Do you serve an ungodly house? So did Obadiah where Jezebel ruled.'[15] Wigram particularly warned against 'the defect of mannerisms' and 'a non-natural style'. On this point Wigram offered a brief vignette of an affected clergyman:

> Whether from shyness in public or from mistaken taste, he is unnatural in the house of God. He is stiff and formal in style and address. He has a preacher manner and his preaching voice ... He seems to leave his ordinary and real self when he enters his public work.'[16]

Wigram's advice was to be 'thoroughly natural in all we say or do'. It is, he asserted, 'a great requirement in these days of science and art'. Earnestness, simplicity, clear words, bright figures and illustrative facts were, in his view, the way to people's hearts.[17] Clergy must avoid preaching 'a pulpit essay'.[18] He reminded his hearers of the great strength of Methodism, which 'gave religion a familiar dress',[19] and stressed that like them our message must address the issues of daily life.

From Jesus and his followers Wigram stated we learn a number of vital lessons. Their preaching was always direct. Jesus used the plainest and most familiar manner of speech. He delighted in parables and figurative language and his illustrations were deep. The Lord and his disciples showed 'tender consideration for the peculiar condition of their hearers'. They were humble and 'did not seek their own glory'. Their animating principle was 'love of souls.'[20] Wigram concluded his concerns about preaching by stating that the earnest preacher would choose a subject appropriate to the times, select a text bearing on the subject, start preparing at the beginning of the week, take the sermon with him and meditate on it, read things relevant to it and stir up the gift of the Spirit in himself.[21] To fuel our preaching we should all of us 'have some topics for study in hand' and 'then in time they will come to inform our preaching.'[22]

ORDINATIONS

Wigram was ever diligent when it came to the matter of ordinations. He was particularly concerned to ensure that all those presenting themselves for ordination should be able to demonstrate an ability to read the liturgy well and 'without an affected or monotonous voice.'[23] The *Kentish Gazette* reported that he required all candidates for holy orders to have the 'power of voice sufficient for his public ministrations.'[24] In September 1860 *The Rochester, Chatham and Strood Gazette* intimated that Wigram would be holding a general ordination on 28 December and had issued the following notice, 'Candidates for ordination are requested to bear in mind that the objects of the examination will be to ascertain their acquaintance with the subjects especially needed for the duties of their holy calling, rather than the contents of any particular books'. The paper then went on to spell out the topics on which candidates were to be examined.

> 1. The Old Testament, historically and doctrinally, and especially in its connection with the New Testament. 2. The whole of the Greek Testament; a fair and competent critical knowledge of the Greek text will be required. 3. The evidences of Christianity as treated by Paley, including the Horae Paulinae, Archbishop Sumner, and as deducible from Butler's Analogy. 4. Ecclesiastical History, especially the first four centuries, Robertson's Church History. 5. History of the English Church, especially at the Reformation, Bishop Short's History of the Church, Blunt's History of the Reformation. 6. The Prayer Book, its history and doctrine: especially the Thirty-Nine Articles, Bishop Beveridge, Professor Harold Browne; The Creed, Offices & co, Bishop Pearson, Hooker, 5th book. 7. The Pastoral Office, Bishop Burnet's Pastoral Care, Herbert's Country Pastor, Blunt's Duties of a Parish Priest. 8. The Latin Tongue, Grotius de Veretate, Jewel's Apologia.[25]

Considering the demanding nature of this examination it is surprising that Wigram appears to have had quite a large number of candidates at his ordination services. He did, in fact, hold his first ordination in Rochester Cathedral on 28 December 1860, as the newspaper had intimated. Ten candidates were made deacons and seven ordained as priests. All but two had received their education at either Oxford of Cambridge.[26] He held a second ordination at Chelmsford on 7 July 1861.[27] Four years later in his second Charge to the clergy in the autumn of 1864 Wigram stated that he had received 133 candidates for the ministry since 1860. Of these, 103 were university men, 19 from King's College, London, 10 from other colleges.[28] Wigram was of the view that 'University training, following upon good school discipline, is an immense advantage', but noted that 'in respect of the examination for orders the non-university men commonly do well, often very well'. He was gratified that very efficient men had joined the ministry from the army and the navy and brought the 'discipline and gentlemanly bearing of their professions to tell with effect in aid of the sacred cause'.[29]

CONFIRMATIONS

During his years as rector of St Mary's Church, Southampton Wigram had taken confirmation seriously and had held regular instruction and advertised classes for both young people and adults. Now as bishop he pressed on his clergy the importance of preparing young people in particular for confirmation in their local parishes. He considered this to be a vital means of bringing them to a personal faith in Christ and becoming actively involved in the life of the church. Local press reports give occasional glimpses of what some of these occasions may have been like.

Soon after becoming bishop, Wigram visited Colchester and was met by the mayor and town council, who offered their congratulations on his appointment, and he went on to visit the 'Camp Church', where he confirmed 390 soldiers.[30] In March 1862 *The Essex Weekly News* carried an article entitled 'Confirmation at Romford'. It took place in St Edward's Church, which 'notwithstanding the unfavourable weather was completely filled'. It must have been an impressive spectacle since the paper reported 'there were three to four thousand people present'.

Pastor of the Clergy and People

As his Lordship arrived in the town at about three o'clock the church bells immediately began ringing. Carriages, cabs, omnibuses and other vehicles soon started arriving in force at the church doors and in a very short time every available space from which a sight of the ceremony could be obtained was occupied. Wigram entered the building at four o'clock and the service proceeded in the usual form. It began with a confirmation hymn, after which the Litany was read by his nephew, the Revd S. Wigram of Romford. Bishop Wigram then addressed a few encouraging remarks to the candidates before proceeding to the laying on of hands. A total of 261 candidates were confirmed with Romford supplying 142 females and 75 boys.[31]

On 3 May 1863 *The Chelmsford Chronicle* reported that the Lord Bishop of Rochester visited 'an exceedingly well-filled' St Peter's Church, Colchester 'for the purpose of performing the ceremony of confirmation'. Ten clergy were present along with candidates from their parishes. After the singing of a hymn, the Litany was read by the Revd H. Cadell, the vicar of St Peter's. The Bishop then delivered a short but impressive address. He then proceeded to the Communion rails and administered confirmation to about 200 young people.[32]

It soon becomes clear that Wigram's confirmation services must have been taxing, to say the least. At a conference with his clergy shortly after delivering his first Charge he announced his intention to hold all his confirmations annually in the spring. In this way they could make full use of the lighter evenings and would avoid the busy harvest period. *The Kentish Gazette* published his confirmation schedule for the spring of 1861, and it was a demanding one to say the least.

> Thursday, Friday, and Saturday, February 21st, 22nd, and 23rd, for confirming in the deaneries of Rochford Hundred. MARCH:— Wednesday 6th, at Barnet and Watford; Thursday, 7th, Kings Langley and Rickmansworth; Friday, 8th, Hemel Hampstead and Great Birkhampstead; Saturday, 9th, Tring and Redburn; Sunday, 10th, for the parishes of St Alban's, in Abbey Church; Monday, 11th, Hatfield and Wheathamstead; Tuesday, 12th, Welwyn and Stevenage; Wednesday, 13th, Hitchin and Baldock; Thursday, 14th, Therfield near Royston; Friday 15th, Barkway and Great Hormead; Saturday, 16th, Cottered and Walton; Monday, 18th, Hertford and Ware; Wednesday, 20th, Broxbourne and Waltham Abbey;

Joseph Cotton Wigram

> Saturday, 23rd, Milton-next-Gravesend; Monday, 25th, Rochester Cathedral; Wednesday, 27th, Colchester. APRIL:—Thursday, 4th, Harlow, at Bishop Stortford; Friday, 5th, Much Hadham; and shortly afterwards at Great Chesterford, Saffron Walden, Witham, Southminster, and Tillingham.[33]

In his much later memoir, Canon O. W. Davys, rector of Wheathampstead, remembered Wigram's visit to his church for a confirmation, 'only a few weeks before his sudden death'. He 'stayed with us for it', wrote Davys, 'and I am glad to say expressed himself much pleased with the work we had done'.[34]

COUNSEL AND ADVICE

Despite his huge workload and constant travel, Wigram was diligent and careful in the advice he offered to his clergy and wise in the commendations and rebukes which from time to time he found it necessary to raise against their misdemeanours. These are seen in some of his letters held in the Lambeth Palace Library and provide us with glimpses and insight into Wigram's wisdom, judgement and character. For example, on 30 May 1861 he wrote a reply to the Bishop of London, Archibald Tait, which demonstrated these qualities. Tait had asked for a commendation on behalf of the Revd W. Watson, who had held a living in his Rochester diocese. Wigram began by stating it would be difficult to give a brief response even though he had known of Watson in the past, when he ran 'a most respectable school in Brighton and had educated one of his brother's boys'. However, on his coming to Rochester Wigram found him involved in a suit for adultery in the Dudley Ryder case. 'It seemed to me unquestionable', Wigram wrote, 'that he was better away from Ickleford, where Mrs D. Ryder resided, apart from her husband, and continued to attend church, play the organ and use every influence she could.' Wigram went on to report that 'things were in a wretched state' and eventually, after speaking with the Archbishop, he removed Watson's license for three years' and told him that he must not ask for a license in the Rochester diocese again. The events that followed convinced Wigram that he had acted rightly and he ended his letter to Tait stating, 'I should be glad to know that he had had an opportunity of recovering himself, but under the circumstances I do not feel at liberty to take the responsibility of recommending his appointment anywhere.'[35]

In October the following year Wigram responded to a request from the Archbishop of York for a reference for Francis Jones, a curate of Braintree, for a curacy in the diocese of York. He replied stating, 'I have great difficulty in countersigning his testimonials'. The reason was that two neighbouring rural deans had given 'unfavourable reports' of Jones's ministry.[36] In September 1864 Wigram replied to another request from Bishop Tait, who in this instance had enquired as to the suitability of Mr Nicholson, who had ministered at St Edward's, Romford, which was then in the Rochester diocese. Wigram had no personal knowledge of Nicholson but took the trouble to find out what he could, discovering in the process that Nicholson had never been properly licensed and during his short time in the parish had created 'a sensation'. Wigram wrote that he had been informed that 'Nicholson's bias is decidedly high' and, if left to himself, 'he would probably go to some extremes'. It also appeared that 'he didn't get on nicely with the parochial clergy and there was jealousy of anyone placed above him'. Wigram had also learned that Nicholson was Irish, from the neighbourhood of Armagh, and fluent in speech with a commanding manner in the pulpit. 'But the clergy of the place', Wigram stated, 'agreed there was very little matter or power in his sermons though they were often clever and authoritative.' Wigram clearly felt he had written more than enough for Tait to make a decision and simply ended thanking him for the kindness of his recent letters.[37]

A somewhat different issue caused Wigram to protest to Tait that the Revd Waldron, a licensed clergyman in his London diocese, had had the 'indiscretion—the term is too mild—to administer the Lord's Supper in New Barnet Church in my diocese, being only in deacon's orders'. It turned out that Waldron had been invited by the churchwarden to cover two Sundays, which turned out to be six. On one of the Sundays the congregation had come expecting to have communion administered and Waldron didn't want to disappoint them. Wigram found that he had been a respectable student at King's

College and then stated, 'I have prohibited Mr Waldron from taking duty in my diocese again.'[38]

Other extant letters from Wigram's pen contain positive views and commendations of his clergy who were needing support or looking for positions in other dioceses. Writing to Bishop Tait in November 1861 he was happy to commend Mr Buckworth-Bailey for the appointment at Yokohama. The testimony concerning him, Wigram reported, 'was very satisfactory, as were the persons who gave it; they are all good men'. He himself recalled once meeting Buckworth-Bailey in Waltham Abbey Church and was 'there confirmed in the good opinion I had framed.'[39] In July 1863 Wigram wrote to the curate of Welwyn, the Revd Bryan Crowther, that he was happy to sign his testimonials to the Bishop of Gibraltar. He went on to speak of 'the satisfaction I have had in witnessing your discharge of the pastoral duties incumbent on you since the summer of 1860'. He added, 'I see your license dates from September 1856. I believe you have been faithful, diligent and efficient in your ministrations during the whole of that period.'[40] He followed this with a letter to Tait, who had pastoral oversight of congregations in Europe, with a similar report stating that Crowther 'is a worthy son of worthy parents whose incumbent gave me a good account of him stating that he manifested an excellent feeling by cheerfully complying with whatever was clearly his duty though opposed to his worldly advantage.'[41]

Wigram was similarly warm in a letter he sent from Danbury Palace to the Revd G. P. Sutton, who was seeking to take up a position in Corfu. He expressed his satisfaction on receiving a note of commendation from the Revd Mr Tamley, Sutton's incumbent, a clergyman whom he had known all his life. Wigram wrote, 'I hope and I expect that the climate of Corfu will suit you and that you may be an instrument in the hands of God for doing good to many. My experience of you both at your ordination and subsequently leads me to expect as much.'[42]

In May 1863 the Revd A. Armstrong of Willesden in the diocese of London and the Revd A. J. Warleigh of St Andrew's, Hertford approached their respective bishops with a request to exchange parishes. Wigram wrote to Tait asking, 'whether Mr Armstrong is a satisfactory clergyman in his parish and without reproach as to conduct'? He was, in the same letter, able to state that 'Mr Warleigh has been long known to me in the Isle of Wight as deserving of such testimony. He is a man of considerable powers in the pulpit, and otherwise'.[43] Among other issues which feature in the correspondence are complaints about an incumbent's excessive playing of the church organ to the annoyance of a section of the parishioners,[44] the non-residence of the Revd J. Watson of Salcot,[45] the Revd W. Thompson's absence from his living for a year due to ill-health but 'jobbing' (taking services) on Sundays.[46] Wigram himself came under scrutiny in the autumn of 1864, when he appointed his nephew, the Revd Spencer Wigram to the living of Prittlewell. Some in the diocese accused him of nepotism. Complaints were made in the press that there were many men of wisdom and experience whilst Wigram had only served as a curate at St Edward's, Romford. One correspondent, signing himself as 'ONE WHO KNOWS PRITTLEWELL', wrote to *The Evening Standard* asking, among other things, 'What are the special qualifications of the Revd Spencer Wigram over and above his relationship to the bishop which have caused him (a young man lately ordained), to be preferred to either the present curate or others of long-standing in the diocese'?[47] His concerns were echoed by *The Atlas*.[48] However, *The Kentish Gazette* and *The Essex Standard* came to his defence, the former pointing out that the income was very small and there was no parsonage or school house. 'The population', it added, 'is a very poor one; so that it is necessary that the incumbent should be a person of considerable private means.'[49] *The Essex Standard* added its pennyworth to the bishop's cause reminding its readers that 'the church is also in a very dilapidated condition, and will require the expenditure of many thousand pounds to restore it'.[50]

Included among the Tait Papers at Lambeth Palace is a letter sent to Wigram from his sister-in-law, Mrs Strange, who was residing with her husband in Naples. She wrote to say that 'the British Consul Mr Bonham told us yesterday that Mr Pugh has sent in his resignation as chaplain'. 'The residents here', she continued, 'have long been tired of Mr Pugh' and 'there is a longing for a thoroughly pious evangelical English clergyman.' 'It is also wished', she stated, 'that a man of experience and good judgement should be appointed.' In particular they need 'a good preacher and a truly consistent Christian'. If such a person isn't found she fears that the members of this church of the Church of England in

Joseph Cotton Wigram

this foreign land will desert to the Presbyterians. She ends, 'Can you say a word for our cause to the Bishop of London as you are so intimate with his Lordship'?[51] Wigram duly complied with her request in a letter to Tait dated 17 April 1861. He enclosed his sister-in-law's letter stating 'it is not meant for your eyes but may do service in showing the feeling which prevails in Naples and the nature and value of the appointment which I presume rest with you. Pray destroy it afterwards'.[52]

FAMILY LIFE

No full descriptions of life in the Wigram household have come to light but the available evidence suggests it was a warm, socially active and happy environment. Clergy in his diocese spoke of his warm outgoing personality and his welcoming manner. He was a strong believer in the importance of a good home environment and was known for his generous hospitality. He also set high store on family prayers and daily reading of the Scriptures in the home. A man of considerable wealth, with a prominent position in society and a large family to bring up, Wigram and his wife maintained a sizeable establishment of servants and staff at their Danbury estate. The 1861 census records twelve living-in servants at the Palace, including a butler, housekeeper, and numerous maids, though no one actually called a cook. Other servants included a coachman, groom and gardener.*

Wigram and his wife had a full, busy and cordial family life. They had ten children all of whom survived into adulthood with the exception of Arthur, who died at the age of two during their time at East Tisted.[53] The marriage at Danbury of their eldest daughter, Susan Caroline, to Major George Clowes of the 8th Hussars, on 20 June 1861, was covered in some detail by *The Chelmsford Chronicle*. The bride's father officiated and, in the words of the *Chronicle*, the service was 'most impressively performed'. The family breakfast which followed lacked nothing 'that

---

* Among the visitors staying at the Palace on census night (7 April) were several of Mrs Wigram's Arkwright relatives. Wigram himself was absent. He was staying with the Revd Lord Charles Hervey, Vicar of Great and Little Chesterford, two Essex parishes in the diocese of Rochester.

could contribute to comfort and enjoyment; and the skilful disposition of fruit and flowers was most pleasing to the eye', the 'size and condition of the grapes from his lordship's own vineries' attracting the 'highest commendation'.[54]

The Wigram's relationship was clearly warm and intimate since their tenth child, Eustace Rochester (1860–1940), was born when Wigram was in his sixty-second year. Sadly, his wife died just two years later on Monday, 27 June 1864, following a sudden and painful attack of pleurisy, which had only begun on the previous Wednesday. At the time she was on a visit to her Arkwright relatives at Mark Hall, Latton. *The Chelmsford Chronicle* provided this moving tribute in her memory.

> It is with a feeling of deep sorrow that we record an event which has already called forth the most painful feelings and no ordinary degree of sympathy in this county, and will cause wide regret in all those who will now first learn it from our columns—the sudden death of Mrs Wigram, the wife of the Lord Bishop of Rochester. All who had been brought within the circle of her influence since her residence in Essex had seen how well she understood and discharged the social and sacred duties that devolve on the wife of a chief ruler of the church; all in this district had learned to appreciate her kind and benevolent spirit; and we trust it will not be deemed an unseemly intrusion, when we tender, as we have been requested to do by many who forbear to approach him formally in this hour of sorrow, the general sympathy felt for our Right Rev. Diocesan, not only among churchmen, but all classes in the county, in his deep domestic affliction.[55]

Susan Wigram was buried in Latton churchyard in a vault on the eastern side, next to that of her aunt Anne Wigram. Inscribed in the front of Wigram's Bible are the following words, which bespeak his strong faith and deep spirituality in this moment of crisis: 'The Lord gave the Lord hath taken away. Blessed be the name to the Lord'. 'She walked with God and was not, for God took her.' 'Absent from the body she is present with the Lord.' 'To die is gain.' 'To be with Christ is far better.' 'Blessed be the dead which die in the Lord. They rest from all their labours.' 'Jesus said, "Because I live, ye shall live also"'. 'My hope, my joy, my crown of rejoicing in the presence of our Lord Jesus Christ at his coming'.[56] *The Essex Weekly News* noted that Wigram was unable take his expected

Joseph Cotton Wigram

role at the re-opening of Earls Colne Church on account 'of his recent heavy bereavement in the unexpected death of Mrs Wigram'. His place was taken by the Right Revd Bishop of Columbia, John Sheepshanks.[57]

Wigram's faith was doubtless challenged by this sudden loss of his loving and supporting wife at a relatively young age. However, he was a man of deep resolve, courage and determination and seems to have resumed his many responsibilities within a relatively short time. Indeed, later in the year he put together his *Second Charge to the Clergy of the Diocese*.

DENOUEMENT

Lord Palmerston, prompted by Lord Shaftesbury, had sought to move away from appointing bishops who were High Church and scholarly in the mould of Howley, Hinds and Blomfield. On the whole he selected men who had themselves worked in parishes and knew the conditions of the working classes from first-hand personal acquaintance. The majority of the Palmerstonian bishops were first and foremost pastors of the people, Wigram among them. He was no mean scholar, but his pastoral skills played out in all his parochial work and particularly so in his episcopacy. In this he was clearly guided and prompted by his deep personal evangelical faith. He always made prayer a priority in his own life and constantly urged his clergy to do the same. He wrote books of devotion and he had a deep knowledge of the Bible, which was particularly evident in his preaching and theological writings.[58]

In his book *The Diocesan Revival*, Arthur Burns argues that diocesan reform began to take place well before the 1830s with the revival of the office of rural dean and the creation of diocesan societies.[59] Somehow the diocese of Rochester in Wigram's time doesn't sit comfortably with this assertion. Straddling the Thames, it was large and unwieldly (see page 64), and Wigram lived out in Essex and kept a house in London. There is little evidence that people had a sense of diocesan consciousness or that the people around Rochester Cathedral felt a strong bond with the farm labourers of north Hertfordshire. In fact, speaking in the Upper House of Convocation in February 1865 Wigram stated;

Pastor of the Clergy and People

> With regard to the diocese of Rochester I believe that its division would be most acceptable in the diocese itself. I am constantly embarrassed by the inconvenience which arises from the form of my diocese; the clergy on the Rochester side frequently do not allow their wants to be known on account of the labour and fatigue which attention to them would involve, and the consequence is that I am deprived of those opportunities for usefulness which every bishop must desire to have.[60]

Wigram went on to relate that when the subject of dividing the diocese had been mooted earlier with reference to the establishment of a bishopric at St Albans, the gentry of Hertfordshire subscribed a substantial sum to facilitate the division, but they were 'discouraged from proceeding further' and withdrew half the money. (The remaining half was used to restore the Abbey at St Albans.) That said, things moved slowly and it wasn't until the diocese was subdivided with formation of St Albans in Hertfordshire in 1877 and, much later, Chelmsford in Essex in 1914 that there were small enough territories capable of developing bonds of unity and consciousness. It wasn't until Bishop Harold Browne, another Palmerstonian bishop, summoned the first Diocesan Conference in 1865, with others following soon after, that real diocesan reform and decision making could begin in earnest.

Notes

1. Burgon 1888, vol. 2, pp. 238–9.
2. Palmerston, letter to Queen Victoria, 2 December 1860, in Benson and Esher 1908.
3. *The Chelmsford Chronicle*, 19 April 1867.
4. *The Saturday Review*, 29 December 1860, p. 829.
5. *The Chelmsford Chronicle*, 2 January 1863.
6. *The Rochester, Chatham and Strood Gazette*, 2 October 1860.
7. *The Chelmsford Chronicle*, 16 August 1861.
8. Davys [1912], p. 73.
9. J. C. Wigram, *How to Preach*, 1859, p. 21.
10. Ibid., Title page.
11. Ibid., p. 1.
12. Ibid., p. 5.
13. Ibid., p. 21.
14. Ibid., p. 24.

15 *Ibid.*, pp. 27–8
16 *Ibid.*, p. 34.
17 *Ibid.*, pp. 39–40.
18 *Ibid.*, p. 56.
19 *Ibid.*, p. 43.
20 *Ibid.*, pp. 15–17.
21 *Ibid.*, p. 25.
22 *Ibid.*, p. 59.
23 *The Christian Observer*, August 1862.
24 *The Kentish Gazette*, 24 September 1861.
25 *The Rochester, Chatham and Strood Gazette*, 18 September 1860.
26 *The Chelmsford Chronicle*, 28 December 1860.
27 *Ibid.*, 28 June 1861.
28 *Ibid.*, 3 February 1865.
29 *Ibid.*
30 *The Rochester, Chatham and Strood Gazette*, 5 June 1860.
31 *The Essex Weekly News*, 28 March 1862.
32 *The Chelmsford Chronicle*, 3 April 1863.
33 *The Kentish Gazette*, 12 February 1861.
34 Davys [1912], p. 73.
35 J. C. Wigram, letter to the Bishop of London, 30 May 1861. LPL, Tait Papers, MS 402.
36 J. C. Wigram, letter to the Archbishop of York, 2 October 1862. LPL, Tait Papers, MS 23.
37 J. C. Wigram, letter to the Bishop of London, 27 September 1864. LPL, Tait Papers, MS 291
38 J. C. Wigram, letter to the Bishop of London, 21 January 1867, LPL, Tait Papers, MS 151.
39 J. C. Wigram, letter to the Bishop of London, 20 November 1861, LPL, Tait Papers, MS 417.
40 J. C. Wigram, letter to the Revd J. Bryan Crowther, 2 July 1863, LPL, Tait Papers, MS 292.
41 J. C. Wigram, letter to the Bishop of London, 24 December 1863, LPL, Tait Papers, MS 304.
42 J. C. Wigram, letter to the Revd G. P. Sutton, 1 September 1864, LPL, Tait Papers, MS 162.
43 J. C. Wigram, letter to the Bishop of London, 15 May 1863, LPL, Tait Papers, MS 226.
44 J. C. Wigram, letter to the Revd W. I. Watson, 4 July 1860, LPL, Tait Papers, MS 428.
45 J. C. Wigram, letter concerning the Revd J. Watson, 30 July 1863 (recipient's name is not clear), LPL, Tait Papers, MS 170.

Pastor of the Clergy and People

46 J. C. Wigram, letter to the Bishop of London, 15 October 1864, LPL, Tait Papers, MS 85.
47 *The Evening Standard* [London], 12 October 1864.
48 *The Atlas*, 15 October 1864.
49 *The Kentish Gazette*, 1 November 1864.
50 *The Essex Standard*, 14 October 1864.
51 Mrs Strange, letter to Bishop Wigram, 5 April 1861, LPL, Tait Papers, MS 330.
52 J. C. Wigram, letter to the Bishop of London, 17 April 1861, LPL, Tait Papers, MS 328.
53 Arthur Henry Wigram died 19 April 1842 (date from Joseph Cotton's Bible).
54 *Supplement to the Chelmsford Chronicle*, 5 July 1861.
55 *The Chelmsford Chronicle*, 1 July 1864.
56 Copy of the inscriptions kindly provided by Canon Sir Clifford Wigram Bt.
57 *The Essex Weekly News*, 15 July 1864.
58 See for example, *The Jews, The Appointed Witnesses for God* (1855) and 'The Advent of the Lord The Present Glory of the Church' (1851).
59 See A. Burns 1999.
60 *The Chelmsford Chronicle* 17 February 1865.

8

Evangelical Convictions

PERSONAL RELIGION

Joseph Cotton Wigram was a Christian leader with a deep personal faith in Christ. The spirituality of his life's journey had from the beginning been rooted in prayer and 'searching the Scriptures daily'.[1] Biblical truth was never far from his mind. His sermons were based on it, his charges were informed by it, his counsels were guided by it and his conversations punctuated by it. In fact, he told the clergy of the Winchester Archdeaconry, 'The more spiritual our minds the more influential will our converse be'. And, that 'hearts truly touched with the love of God, will communicate light and heat to others whether they know it or not'.[2] Wigram saw clearly that 'to be effective in ministry our sufficiency must not be by might, nor by power, but by the Spirit'.[3]

Following the practice of the early Methodists many nineteenth-century Evangelicals kept journals and diaries to enable them to reflect on their spiritual disciplines, acknowledge their weaknesses, record steps taken and lessons learned. It is likely that Wigram practised some kind of journaling since he recommended that all his clergy purchase a large book. In it he suggested they write 'the words of the wise' who have gone before us in the church' and references to Scripture concerning the responsibilities of the ministry'. Such Wigram suggested, will be a 'permanent help and comfort in the work of the ministry'.[4]

Joseph Cotton Wigram

PROTESTANT THEOLOGY

Wigram's faith was deeply rooted in the teaching of the sixteenth-century reformers and the theology of the *Book of Common Prayer* and the *Articles of Religion*. He frequently reminded both liberals and ritualists of the need to adhere to the teaching 'of the reformed the Church of England'. He spoke in his second Charge to his diocesan clergy of the great importance of the Reformation 'which had mercifully delivered our nation from the practices of the corrupt Roman system'. 'It is a system', he said, 'as little suited to the wants of our time as it is consistent with the simplicity and spirituality of Christ's religion.'[5] Wigram was adamant that neither he nor any of his diocesan clergy should 'leave the old paths, and quit the trodden ways'. He urged them to keep their focus on 'the most simple doctrines of repentance from dead works, of faith towards God, of the resurrection of the dead and of judgement to come'. 'These', he continued, 'are the foundations and corner-stones on which we build, from the very beginning, our sure and blessed hope.'[6]

Wigram had a strong belief in the inspiration of Scripture and frequently referred to the Bible as 'the Word of God'.[7] In a Lenten address in 1850 he summed up his personal faith in the following way, 'The Evangelical spirit of our reformed church, requires that its members should be encouraged to search the Scriptures daily for ... the dignity of the Saviour's person, the marvel of his incarnation, the value of his atonement, the nature of his eternal priesthood and the efficacy of His intercession'.[8] He then added that 'the blessed hope, and glorious appearing of the great God and our Saviour Jesus Christ ... will inaugurate the consummation of that blessedness for which his faithful ones look'.[9] Wigram advocated that the words of Scripture should 'be received with a humble child-like reception'.[10] He maintained that the inspiration of Scripture 'was seen in the unity and harmony in the varied portions of its revelation'. It was this coherence which he saw running through the Old and New Testament that 'imparts in me a response of peaceful confidence'.[11]

Evangelical Convictions

THE HOLY SPIRIT

Wigram began the introduction to his first Charge to the clergy of the diocese by urging them to unite 'to implore the Holy Spirit, who alone can help our infirmities, and by His quickening power make us strong to strengthen others in the faith'.[12] He ended it by praying that the Lord by His Spirit 'will build you up in your most holy faith, and make you able for every good work! Breathe Lord! Breathe forth the life-giving power of the Holy Ghost on each and every heart'!... And hasten the day when Thy Spirit shall be put into every heart, that all shall know Thee, from the least to the greatest'!'[13]

ATONEMENT

In his very first sermon in Rochester Cathedral following his consecration he emphasised that 'Jesus was the sacrifice for our sins, and offered himself up, as we, believing in him and trusting in his intercession, are to lay our sins on him and carry out the simplicity of that delightful hymn—

> My faith would lay her hand
> On that dear head of Thine,
> While like a penitent I stand
> And there confess my sin.

Christ's intercession, Wigram stressed 'is still ongoing' as he stands as the mediator between God and men.[14] In December 1863 Wigram issued a pastoral circular to his rural deans, in which he suggested that they organise deanery meetings 'to instruct people in the solid grounds of the Christian faith'. Prominent among the topics he advocated were 'the authenticity and inspiration of Holy Scripture' and 'the nature and efficacy of the atonement of Christ'.[15]

Joseph Cotton Wigram

THE CHURCH

In the same address Wigram reminded the congregation that the church is a 'spiritual building' and composed of 'living stones'. The real disciples of Jesus were 'animated by a principle of life received from Him'. When he moved on to speak of the role of the clergy, he posed a rhetorical question, 'But where are the priests'? In response he said, 'They are all the household of faith. The people of God were a priesthood. And this was no new notion'. Wigram then explained that Exodus 19 teaches us that God's people were made a kingdom of priests and that St Peter called all Christians 'a royal priesthood'. If anyone should ask, 'how is it that believers can be priests'? Wigram's answer was 'God knows if we don't' and he added, 'St John says, "We shall be kings and priests with God"'. 'There is', he continued, 'a ministry for everyone to perform in their own vocation as they offer up their souls and bodies to God which is our reasonable service.'[16] From this premise it is abundantly clear the Wigram's understanding of the nature of the clerical office and ministry was very far from anything approaching the doctrine of 'apostolic successions' being taught by the Oxford Movement whereby the spirit of the first apostles was passed down through successive generations by the laying on of episcopal hands at ordination. The clergyman was in no way ontologically different from the layman by virtue of his ordination. His function was to be a steward of God's word to feed the flock and a pastor of God's people.[17] For the laity, as St Peter put it, everyone has received a gift and should 'minister the same to one another, as good stewards of the manifold grace of God'. In still bolder imagery, the apostle declared 'there is a "priesthood" pertaining to all who believe, and there are "sacrifices" which all are to offer up'.[18] In view of this it comes as no surprise that Wigram was totally committed to the ministry of lay men and lay women.

He concluded the matter stressing that 'we minister to souls! Souls! Methinks, in that one word, there is a sermon. Immortal souls! Immortal souls! One whereof is more worth than all the world besides, the price of the blood of the Son of God.'[19] This challenges us not to be idle 'but to lay ourselves at God's feet, arise and do the work of God with all faithfulness and industry'.[20]

Evangelical Convictions

THE GOSPEL

Wigram's entire life and ministry was focused on proclaiming the Gospel message by word of mouth and practical caring ministry. In his first Charge to the clergy of the diocese he declared, 'And what my heart longs for is—a system pervading the length and breadth of the land, whereby every man, in his own private walk in life, is quietly but energetically doing his utmost to diffuse the blessed influences of Gospel truth'.[21]

We must, he exhorted the clergy, create an instrumentality to achieve 'the evangelizing of the whole body of the people, the leavening of the mass of society with a better spirit than now possesses it'.[22] Such, he opined, 'must be the work of the holy Spirit upon the hearts of men'. Towards the end of this, his first Charge, he returned to supreme importance of bringing people to faith in the Gospel. Constrained by the love of Christ the clergyman is 'to make himself the servant of all' and 'be spent for the souls which have been redeemed by His Master's blood'.[23]

ESCHATOLOGY AND THE RETURN OF CHRIST

In 1850 Wigram gave a lecture entitled 'The Advent of the Lord the Present Glory of the Church', which was later published in a volume edited by William Wilson entitled *The Blessings of the Lord's Second Advent*. In it Wigram stressed the day of Christ's coming will be one of 'peculiar resurrection blessedness for the saints'.[24] The blessedness, he asserted, lay in the thousand year reign, in which believers will participate on Christ's return.[25]

Wigram held to a very literal view of the end time period or 'last days'. In another address he spoke of the Jews returning to their land, Jerusalem being exalted over the earth, and David's son occupying 'as he has never done, the promised throne'.[26] Along with a number of Evangelicals, Wigram maintained that the Jewish nation would play a significant role in the last days before Christ's return. In his sermon entitled 'The Jews, the Appointed Witnesses for God in the Successive Ages of the World', preached on behalf of the Operative Jewish Converts' Institution, he declared, 'He who is the "first and the last, the only God", He has called the Hebrew people and declared His purpose towards them, and established them as his witnesses to the world, from the beginning, until now, and even to the end'![27] Wigram asserted that notwithstanding everything that the nation of Israel had passed through

> in all successive ages, under circumstances of every kind, whether the people be in prosperity or distress,—whether in the sunshine of his favour, or under the deep shadow of his wrath,—whether in their delightsome land, or captive and subject to hostile powers, or scattered to every corner of the earth, with every distinction of tribe and inheritance done away and unknown even to themselves,—yet still they should equally continue distinguished from all other people in the world, and yield an unmistakeable evidence to the truth of his purposes and the glory of his name.[28]

Expounding the Old Testament prophecies of Ezekiel chapter 36 and Hosea chapter 3, Wigram was clear that in a future age in the latter days the Lord will take the children of Israel from among the heathen 'and bring them into their own land'.[29] In his concluding words he reiterated the same point, 'Thou wilt bring them back to their father's land,—Jerusalem, thine own city, shall again be exalted, and made very high, even above every other which has or can exist in the earth'.[30] This return of the Jews to Israel and the raising up of Jerusalem, Wigram maintained, will reach a final consummation when the 'new' and 'heavenly Jerusalem comes down out of heaven to earth as a bride betrothed to her husband which is Christ, and there made partakers of married joys'.[31]

Wigram, along with other prominent Evangelicals including the 7th Earl of Shaftesbury and bishops such as Montagu Villiers and Robert Bickersteth, firmly believed that Christ would return and rule the earth for a thousand years before the final ending of the present age. This doctrine, often termed Pre-millennialism, asserted that the Lord's return would be 'pre' or before the millennium, which would be a literal period of a thousand years (millennium being Latin for a thousand years) of bliss on earth. Wigram stated it forthrightly in 'The Advent of the Lord the Present Glory of the Church', which was published in 1851.

Evangelical Convictions

> That period, 'a thousand years' is so frequently and so emphatically repeated in this passage (six times),—it is so connected with those great realities, Christ—Satan—the saints—the rest of the dead—the living on the earth—the reward of heaven—the punishment of sin—the reward of heaven and hell,—that my whole confidence in the Scripture, my hope of reward, would be shaken to the cornerstone, if I could allow myself, as many do (as I myself have done in the past), to allegorize, and in effect to explain it away, this concentration of the prophetic announcements with which the canon of Scripture is closed.[32]

This intense focus on the role of Jerusalem in the last days on the part of Wigram and other Evangelical bishops and clergy led them to be firm supporters of the Anglican bishopric of Jerusalem, which had been established by Britain and Prussia in 1841.[33]

JUDGEMENT AND THE FINAL STATE

Wigram was clear that at the return of Christ 'a general resurrection, both of the just and unjust' would immediately follow.[34] In addition, there will be 'a second resurrection' or 'better resurrection' of the martyrs (Hebrews 11: 35) who will live and reign with Christ on Earth for a thousand years (Revelation 20: 4–5)'.[35] In that moment of the great Advent 'the Saviour, the Lord Jesus Christ shall change our vile body, that it may be like his glorious body'.[36] At the end of the thousand year period the devil will finally be destroyed 'being cast into the lake of fire for ever. And so the judgement is closed'.[37] Wigram had just one further point to add, 'For the blessed who rise unto life there are degrees and orders of blessedness, and varied offices described as entrusted to their hands'.[38]

Wigram's views of the coming judgement and the final states of heaven and hell were those of the evangelical world of his day. In an address to clergy he reminded his hearers that 'the great and awful realities of heaven and hell hold a prominent and permanent place in the faith'.[39] 'The judgement to come', he emphasised, 'is in numerous passages of the Word of God.'[40]

Joseph Cotton Wigram

Wigram's exposition of the last days was clearly a fundamentalist one which interpreted the thousand years with great literalness in terms of physicality and time and without reference to the symbolism in the rest of the Book of Revelation. His stance was characteristic of many of the views expressed in *The Record*. One critic related that he had had the misfortune to hear 'one of these Judaizers advocate the notion that the 'Lost Tribes' are identical with the Saxons on the ground that *Saxon* is an abridgment of Isaac's son'.[41]

LIFESTYLE

Wigram's lifestyle was informed and driven by his Protestant evangelical faith and spirituality. He was a man of prayer whose habits and conduct were constantly informed by his deep knowledge of the Scriptures and his disciplined habits. He had what at times appeared to be a somewhat austere and puritanical side to his character, which he may well have derived from the works of William Law and other pietist writers.[42] This trait, as has been noted in the earlier chapters of this study, led to his strictures against activities which he considered to be 'worldly distractions'. He pronounced against recreations such as horse racing and dancing and urged his clergy not to play for local cricket teams, grow beards or buy the latest fashion clothes. Along with most Evangelicals he kept and advocated a strict Sabbatarian Sunday. In his 1849 Archdiaconal Charge to the clergy and churchwardens of the Archdeaconry of Winchester. Wigram told the wardens it was a prime duty to 'See that the Lord's Day is kept and that no lawless disturbances desecrate the sacred rest'.[43] Wigram fitted perfectly into what Ian Bradley described as 'the Cult of Conduct'. Writing in *The Call to Seriousness*, Bradley observed that 'the Evangelicals had a very high view of the part that the influence and example of others could play in affecting a man's behaviour both for good and ill. They went to considerable lengths to ensure that their contemporaries were spared these influences which were not conducive to sound moralities'.[44]

Evangelical Convictions

DENOUEMENT

W. J. Conybeare in his celebrated article entitled 'Church Parties' observed two categories of Church of England Evangelicals. One group he termed 'The Old Evangelical party'.[45] Their hallmarks, he suggested, were philanthropic work in mines and factories, prison reform, the establishment of Ragged Schools, the founding of the Church Missionary Society (CMS) and the British and Foreign Bible Society (BFBS), and the establishment of Church Building Societies.[46] Their supreme achievement was the suppression of the slave trade. By the mid-nineteenth century Conybeare was of the view that the Moderates were diminishing in influence and hold on the public.[47] 'The Old Evangelicals' tended to favour the opinions put out by *The Christian Observer*. By contrast, Conybeare designated the second strand of Evangelical Anglicans as the 'Recordite Party' after their preferred church periodical *The Record*. They were, he suggested marked out, not by a mere belief in the authority of Scripture, but by a rigid adherence to verbal inspiration. According to the Recordites, 'The Bible is regarded not as a collection of books written by men under divine guidance, but as a single book, dictated in every word by God himself'.[48] Their favourite society was that which professed to be founded for the conversion of the Israelites to Christianity. They taught that the Christian Lord's Day was identical with the Jewish Sabbath and was therefore to be kept with strictness and vigour.

The ministry of a Recordite clergyman, according to Conybeare, was focused on the preaching of two extemporary sermons on Sunday. Their principal concerns were 'the approaching restoration of the Jews, the date of the Millennium, the progress of the 'Tractarian heresy' and the anticipated 'perversion' of High Church neighbours'. Boyd Hilton, writing in 1991, designated 'The Old Evangelicals' as 'The Moderates' and suggested that they generally took a more cheerful view of private and national misfortune, believing, in many cases, it resulted as the natural consequence of misguided error. In contrast the Recordites, whom he designated as 'the Extremists', saw misfortune as having been caused by sin. The Extremists welcomed disaster as a sign of the last days.[49] The Moderates generally had a more cheerful and affirming

Joseph Cotton Wigram

attitude to the pleasures of living than the Extremists. The Moderates, as Hilton observed them, were post-millennialists, who saw the need to build and work towards New Jerusalem. The great majority of the Extremists were pre-millennial and hence believed that social improvement would only materialise after the second coming of Christ. Not surprisingly, therefore, many Extremists became increasingly drawn away from the social activism of the Clapham moderates.

The Moderate Evangelical Anglicans tended to down-play emotional experiences, while in contrast Extremists set much store on prophetic and revivalist campaigns. Again, the Moderates were not antipathetic to scientific discovery,[50] whereas the Recordite Extremists opposed any accommodation to science which conflicted with their interpretation of Scripture. Although the Moderates held the Bible to be inspired, they were not literalists or fundamentalists in the way that the Extremists became in the 1840s.

In the light of this analysis it is clear that Wigram was a Recordite Evangelical. It is true that he was a strong supporter of the CMS and The British and Foreign Bible Society but theologically he clearly identified with the Extremists. He had a strong belief in the inspiration of the Scripture, which he interpreted with great literalness, seen particularly in the role of the Jewish nation in the end times, the imminent coming of Christ and the establishing of his thousand-year reign on earth. Like the Recordites, Wigram had a decidedly Puritanical aspect to his character, as we have seen.

Wigram was not, however, an 'enthusiast' in the sense that the Primitive Methodists or Salvation Army officers were. In a sermon based on St Paul's testimony to King Agrippa he defined 'enthusiasts' as 'those who have been remarkably prone to dwell upon their raptures, and visions and intercourse with God'.[51] He went on to point out that St Paul only ever mentioned his experience of raptures once and that was 'fourteen years after they had happened'.[52] In his sermon Wigram was clear that 'there has been, and still is, much enthusiasm exercised under the name of religion' and that some good men 'had through human frailty been betrayed into excess in religious matters'. His conclusion was that an ardent and zealous spirit is good but does not constitute an enthusiast. In summary it is clear that Wigram was a serious and

Evangelical Convictions

devoted Evangelical who recognised that too much of anything, including religion, is not a good thing. He was a strong believer in keeping a right judgement and exercising moderation in all things.[53]

Notes

1. J. C. Wigram, *The Advent of the Lord*, 1851, p. 28.
2. J. C. Wigram, *Ministerial Watchfulness*, 1845, p. 15.
3. Ibid.
4. Ibid., p. 20.
5. J. C. Wigram, *A Charge ... 1860*, p. 25.
6. J. C. Wigram, *The Advent of the Lord*, 1851, p. 30.
7. Ibid., p. 49 et seq.
8. J. C. Wigram, *The Advent of the Lord*, 1851, p. 24.
9. Ibid., p. 25.
10. Ibid., p. 54.
11. Ibid.
12. J. C. Wigram, *A Charge ... 1860*, p. 3.
13. Ibid., p. 28.
14. *Rochester, Chatham and Strood Gazette*, 12 June 1860.
15. *The Essex Standard*, 16 December 1863.
16. *Rochester, Chatham and Strood Gazette*, 12 June 1860.
17. J. C. Wigram, *A Charge ... 1860*, p. 26.
18. Ibid., p. 13.
19. J. C. Wigram, *Ministerial Watchfulness*, 1845, p. 37.
20. Ibid., p. 38.
21. J. C. Wigram, *A Charge ... 1860*, p. 3.
22. Ibid.
23. Ibid., p. 27.
24. J. C. Wigram, 'The Advent of the Lord', 1851, p. 35.
25. Ibid., p. 53.
26. J. C. Wigram, *The Jews*, 1855, p. 15.
27. Ibid., p. 1.
28. Ibid., p. 5.
29. Ibid., p. 8.
30. Ibid., p. 15.
31. Ibid., p. 18.
32. J. C. Wigram, 'The Advent of the Lord', 1851, p. 53.
33. See Greaves 1949, p. 340.
34. J. C. Wigram, 'The Advent of the Lord', 1851, p. 33.

35 *Ibid.*, p. 36.
36 *Ibid.*, p. 33.
37 *Ibid.*, pp. 40–1.
38 *Ibid.*, p. 42.
39 *Ibid.*, p. 54.
40 *Ibid.*, p. 55.
41 Cited in Bebbington 1989, p. 62.
42 See for example, J. C. Wigram, *On Humility*, p. 7, where he quotes Law's *Serious Call*, chapter 15.
43 J. C. Wigram, *Present Aspects of Popular Educations*, 1849, p. 11.
44 I. Bradley 1976, p. 145.
45 Conybeare 1853, p. 277.
46 *Ibid.*, pp. 277–85.
47 *Ibid.*, p. 283.
48 *Ibid.*, p. 287.
49 Hilton 1991, p. 22.
50 *Ibid.*
51 J. C. Wigram, 'St Paul before King Agrippa', p. 210
52 *Ibid.*
53 *Ibid.*, p. 208.

9

Joseph Cotton Wigram, A Significant Leader

There is no doubt that Joseph Cotton Wigram was a significand nineteenth-century Christian leader. His life deserves to be given recognition for four things in particular. First, he was a prominent educationalist, who played an important part in the national debate over the role of religion in education in the middle years of the nineteenth century. Second, he was a visionary strategist, who was not afraid to challenge the archaic and failing structures of the established church. Third, he was a model and effective parish minster in a sprawling urban quarter of Southampton. Fourth, he was an exemplary missional and pastoral bishop.

A PROMINENT EDUCATIONALIST

Education and the promotion of education at all levels was a constant thread which ran through the whole of Wigram's adult life and ministry. It began most likely in the early days of his curacy at St Mary's, Leyton and its daughter chapel at Leytonstone, where he would have been involved in catechising the young and visiting the village school. It became a much more prominent part of his life when he moved to central London as curate of St James, Westminster in 1827. There, as has been noted, Wigram was responsible for a poverty-stricken section of the parish with its own church, St Luke's, Berwick Street. His deep involvement in the lives of these people, whom William Booth, the founder of the Salvation Army, called 'the sub-merged tenth', made him acutely concerned to raise the level of their education. At precisely the same time that Wigram was ministering among the poor in Westminster (1827–39), he was also undertaking a demanding national role as General Secretary to the National Society for Promoting the Education of the Poor. As a scholar himself he was able to debate the issues and the needs of education with the government of the time with an understanding which came from a daily personal experience at grass-roots level.

The period of Wigram's residence in Westminster was one of change, in which successive governments were trying to secularise the nation's education by loosening the church's long held control over local schools. By contrast Wigram and the Church of England's National Society's schools held steadfastly to the view that the Christian faith and its moral principles must always remain the bedrock and foundation stone of all education. Wigram, as has been clearly seen, constantly championed and argued the cause with the government and the Treasury, which was responsible for making grants for the building and improvement of schools. Wigram was a strong advocate of Model Schools, where good practice could be observed and developed. Even after he had left Westminster, he continued the battle against secularism with untiring focus and resolve. He titled his 1849 Charge to the clergy and churchwardens of the Archdeaconry of Winchester *Present Aspects of Popular Education*. In it he reminded any of the faint-hearted who were listening to him that all National Society schools were committed to the view that 'the secular must not be separated from the religious'. The Society, he continued, 'could only recognise the national religion as the basis for the people's education'.[1]

During his many years as Archdeacon of Winchester Wigram made the Hampshire schools within his archdeaconry a major priority. He frequently organised meetings and training occasions for teachers and gave constant encouragement to clergy to foster and develop their local schools. He was also a major figure in the promotion of Sunday Schools and published *Practical Hints on the Formation and Management of Sunday-Schools*, which went through three editions between 1833 and 1840. His *Geography of the Holy Land* published in 1832 had four editions the last being in 1855. At the very least it should be said that

A Significant Leader

Wigram was a significant figure in the education of the nineteenth century. As a bishop, Wigram took particular care in choosing inspectors for diocesan National schools and gave much support to work of the Rochester Diocese Training College at Hockerill. In summary Wigram must clearly be recognised as a very significant figure in the drive to improve the education of the poor of nineteenth-century England.

A VISIONARY STRATEGIST

When it came to missional action Wigram emerges as an able strategist, who was able to think outside the box. As the rector of the tiny Hampshire living of East Tisted, he recognised the benefits of a working parochial system, which functioned as a small, supportive and caring community in which everyone knew their position and role. However, on his appointment as Archdeacon he suddenly found he was responsible for the ecclesiastical needs of the huge urban sprawl of Portsmouth. So expansive were the growing slums and deprivation that the clergy weren't even beginning to cope with pastoral needs which daily surrounded them. His solution was a bold and imaginative plan, which he published under the title, *The Spiritual Necessities of Portsea*. In this small book he proposed to divide the parish of Portsea into smaller units with assistant clergy being appointed and given pastoral responsibility for their designated areas. Initially, his proposals were only taken on board in a limited way but with the passing of the years there emerged a growing recognition of his foresight and the gradual adoption of his original plan. Wigram was one of the first churchmen to propose breaking down large parishes into smaller pastoral units. His strategy was significant because he had taken deep care to study and analyse the social life and problems of the differing sections of the population. The divisions he put forward were rooted in the social contexts of the population rather than simply being tidy manageable ecclesiastical units on a diocesan map. When he was made rector of St Mary's, Southampton, one of the largest parishes in England, he was able to subdivide his own parish into smaller areas to good and positive effect. Such steps may seem very little when compared with the Fresh

Expressions Movement of the late twentieth century but they were a radical move forward in the middle years of the nineteenth century when the Church of England was hidebound by archaic parliamentary laws, which were difficult and time-consuming to get changed.

A MODEL AND EFFECTIVE PARISH MINISTER

As well as continuing to be an able Archdeacon, Wigram, as has been observed, was a very gifted parish minister. Moving from the rural environment of East Tisted might have come as a shock to his system but his earlier experiences in London, Portsea and other places in his archdeaconry had prepared him for the huge challenge of Southampton's dockland and industrial heartland with its poverty and slums. Wigram had the capacity to spot the big issues and concentrate on them in an efficient manner. Not only was he concerned to support all the schools of the archdeaconry, he made education a major focus in his own parish.

Straightforward practical biblical preaching was a priority along with regular ongoing weekly confirmation and adult education classes. Although a man of considerable wealth, who came from a landed family and believed in a fixed social hierarchy, the poor were never far from Wigram's heart. In Westminster he built up a system of parish visiting, which enabled him to ascertain the needs of the poorest. He took particular care to see that children who were not in school were followed up and brought to book. The parish records of the hamlet parish of East Tisted show Wigram's concern for the small number of village poor. During his episcopate he expressed his particular personal concern for the sailors of the Medway and the large number of soldiers and their families in Colchester, urging clergy and parishes to respond in practical ways their needs.

AN EXEMPLARY AND MISSIONAL BISHOP

The Earl of Shaftesbury had urged on Lord Palmerston the need for bishops who had been active in parish life and who were good pastors.

A Significant Leader

In this matter Wigram was certainly exemplary. He worked with his clergy, valued them, encouraged them and listened to them. He had fifty-two rural deans and constantly asked them to organise meetings of their clergy, which he attended both to listen to their concerns and to speak words of encouragement and exhortation. He enjoyed warm and cordial relationships with his clergy many of whom wrote to support him in times of crisis. This was particularly apparent at the time of the Colenso affair and when his wife died in 1864. On both occasions he responded in the local press to thank all who had written letters of concern support and sympathy.

Wigram's charges to his clergy and the vision and strategy they encapsulated arose out of his listening to them at these and other gatherings. He did not run a top-down hierarchy, rather his strategy was always to work with his clergy. At the beginning of his first Charge in 1860 Wigram wrote that he regarded the meetings with his clergy 'not so much as an opportunity for me to explain my own views, as one at which, after the example of primitive times, you may make known yours to me'. He added that it was his wish that year by year 'this manner of counsel' would continue.[2] All this is not to say that Wigram didn't have suggestions to make or advice to give. He certainly did but it always came as something that might be worth considering or might prove effective in particular locations. They included establishing an evening school, preaching on particular sermon topics, the distribution of tracts or helpful books, starting a small library, improving the quality of harvest homes and having a challenging missionary speaker.

Not only was Wigram concerned for his clergy, he had a particular concern for the laity in every parish. He was a visionary, who believed that not only was it vital that there was a warm and close relationship between all clergy and laity but also that they should work together in every missional enterprise. He went further and was of the view that lay men and women could be involved in almost every aspect of the church's ministry. The use of lay men and particularly lay women in the life and ministry of the church was to become a growing feature in the life and worship of the later Victorian years and in that development Wigram was an obvious forerunner.[3] *The Essex Weekly News* underlined the importance of the periodical conferences between clergy and laity in different parts of the diocese, which were brought about solely by his initiative. They had begun 'to do so much in promoting union in doctrine, discipline and good feeling among the members of the church as well as promoting the welfare, spiritual and temporal, of the poor around them'. 'It is fervently hoped', the correspondent concluded, that 'these gatherings and communings will still go on, and through them the influence of the deceased prelate be long felt in the diocese.' The paper described him as 'emphatically the layman's bishop'.[4]

Wigram was a man who lived what he preached. His critics were few and most likely to be found in the Tractarian and High Church Press, who accused him of being 'small-minded', 'a bishop of little things' and 'the Bishop of Bond Street'.[5] He was described by Bishop Charles Sumner, writing on 15 April 1867, as 'one of the most single-minded, straightforward men I have ever known, somewhat cold in manner, but full of energy and devotion to his work. The diocese will never have a more disinterested and unselfish head'.[6] He was a serious and godly man, who delighted in his wife and family circle. He and his wife were greatly loved by their staff at Danbury Palace as well as people in the local community.

DEATH AND BURIAL

Bishop Wigram died suddenly about 10 o'clock on Saturday night 6 April 1867. He had been holding confirmation services in different parts of the diocese. Having just returned from Rochford in Essex he had arranged to stay overnight in London with family members at his brother's house in Grosvenor Square as he was due to preach at the Chapel Royal, St James's, the next day. In the evening his brother, who was in failing health, had a fainting fit and Wigram helped him up the stairs.[7] Shortly afterwards, when he was in the act of drawing a chair close to the sofa, he fell forward and died without a word. His physician had warned him that the heart condition from which he suffered could result in his sudden death, and a close friend reported that Wigram had had a slight premonition of death about a month earlier, when he nearly fell to the ground. In its account of the bishop's death *The Hertford Mercury* stated, 'it is likely that he was conscious of a coming attack, before he came up to town on Saturday'. 'There is', the paper continued, 'something exceedingly touching in the thought of this excellent prelate going about his appointed duties from day to day, with death constantly in view, suffering nothing to hinder him, while life remained; and it helps us to conceive of the unclouded serenity of his mind.'[8] Wigram had arranged to return to Essex on the Monday to hold confirmation at Braintree.[9]

At the announcement of his death in *The Essex Weekly News* stated that 'few prelates have been more active and indefatigable in the various works he undertook, and in the promotion of all those matters which he considered the responsible duty as a ruler of the church in this district cast upon him'.[10] The paper wrote of 'his earnest attention to duty, his courtesy and his social accessibility for which he was highly esteemed, not only in Essex, but throughout the whole diocese'. It added that all who knew him testified 'to his fitness for his high position, the simplicity of his behaviour and life, his unassuming earnestness, his ready accessibility, his unruffled temper, and his kind heart'.[11] *The Herts Guardian* quoted a comment from *The Times*, that 'Dr. Wigram was an evangelical in his religious views, and a year or two back his somewhat injudicious denunciations *ex cathedra* of those of his clergy who played cricket with their parishioners on village greens, or who wore moustaches and beards, caused no little indignation in Essex and ridicule in London'.[12] For these same reasons *The Saturday Review* dubbed him 'a bishop of little things'.[13] That said, *The Herts Guardian* went on to assert, 'His lordship, however, was a very earnest, hard-working man, without any pretensions to oratorical powers or theological learning; but whatever faults his clergy might find with his discretion, no one ever accused him of discourtesy, inaccessibility, or indifference to the calls of duty'.[14] Despite the rigidity of his views, particularly where ritualism was concerned, such was not the whole story. *Evangelical Christendom* reported that the Revd Brian King, a notorious ritualist, wished to exchange his living, St George's-in-the-East, which had become too hot for him, for one in the Rochester diocese. When Wigram came to know of the request, he offered no obstacle and invited King to spend a few days with him at Danbury Palace so that he might better understand the needs of the proposed new parish. Even *The Pall Mall Gazette* ended its obituary on a conciliatory note, 'We have no wish to be hard on Dr Wigram. There is every evidence of his diligence, sincerity and earnestness'.[15] *The Hertford Mercury* offered this endorsement of Wigram's ministry 'from one who knew him well, and is qualified to speak of his worth': 'Never was a more genial spirit, a more open heart, a more generous mind, a more cheerful piety, blended with firmness in opposing what he believed to be wrong; and when some whom he reproved, because he considered them worthy of blame, spoke openly against him and excited the prejudice of others, he readily forgave and forgot the moment they acknowledged their fault'.[16] The 'one who knew him well' observed two aspects where Wigram failed.[17] First, he was not always careful to set himself right with the public at large. In other words he sometimes failed to justify his actions or correct mistaken misconceptions. He needed to observe the biblical principle not to let his good be evil spoken of. Second, Wigram took on too much. In short, he broke the work–life boundaries, which adversely affected his health and well-being. This was a common fault among many nineteenth-century Evangelicals in all walks of life. They proclaimed a Gospel of grace and freedom, but many were trapped in prisons over-work.

Wigram's funeral took place at Latton Church on 12 April. There was, according to *The Chelmsford Chronicle*, a general feeling among the clergy and leading gentry of the county that they would like to have attended the occasion as a mark of respect for their late diocesan bishop. However, the service was arranged, as Wigram would have wished, with a minimum of public display. It was intended that only near relatives would attend. Those present included two sons, his son-in-law, his three brothers, several relatives of his late wife and some of his servants. Those family members walked the short distance from Mark Hall to the church. In the event a large body of local clergy attended unasked to show respect for their late diocesan. The bishop was laid to rest in a vault in the churchyard where his wife had been buried three years earlier. Wigram left six sons, ranging downward in age from 28 to 7, and three daughters, of whom the eldest was married to Major George Clowes, 'late of the 8th Hussars'.[18]

A Significant Leader

On the Sunday following many clergy gave sermons in which they paid tribute to their bishop's gracious character, labours, leadership and example. Among the many Archdeacon Mildmay gave an impressive tribute in St Mary's Church, Chelmsford. It was based on Matthew 26: 38–9, part of the set reading for the day: 'Then saith he unto them, my soul is exceedingly sorrowful, even unto death: tarry ye here and watch with me. And he went a little further, and fell on his face, and prayed, saying, O, my Father, if it be possible, let this cup pass from me: nevertheless, not as I will, but as thou wilt'.[19] From this Mildmay pointed out how the Saviour had struggled in the garden of Gethsemane beneath the weight and burden of human sin. Then after his final appeal he felt it was the will of the Father and from that moment his whole soul became absorbed in carrying out the will of him who had sent him. In the same way, he pointed out, it often pleased God to call some of his best-chosen instruments as he saw fit to work out his purposes. This might, he suggested, be the reason why 'the most useful, zealous and irreplaceable of God's servants were sometimes suddenly smitten down and taken away', like the bishop, 'in the fulness of his intellect and usefulness, when his work seemed at its best'. Mildmay went on to urge the congregation to be thankful for the so much good work which the bishop, that 'unflinching servant of God', had been permitted to do for his Master's service, and which was so well known to them that he need not dwell on it. He then bore this testimony.

> They could speak of the simplicity of his behaviour and life; of his unassuming earnestness; his ready accessibility; his unruffled temper; his tender heart. They could speak, too, of other qualifications of higher importance. They knew that he spent himself earnestly, indefatigably, and in all singleness of purpose in his Master's cause, and so strong was his ardor in that cause that though again and again warned by the hand of nature of what the consequences would be, he could not be brought to slacken in that labour of love which had become a long habit of his soul. He was sure his works would follow him ... He was, so far as [the people of God's church] might venture to judge, a sincere and earnest christian, and as such they must revere his memory, and give God thanks that he was sent among them though for so short a time.[20]

Joseph Cotton Wigram

The tribute offered in *The Hertford Mercury* fully testified to Wigram's warmth, charm and godly disposition.

> He brought to the performance of episcopal duties few of those brilliant qualities which are thought by some to constitute the highest qualifications; but his fitness was of an infinitely higher kind ... There was a charm in his gentle yet dignified demeanour, which was felt by all; and there was more eloquence in his benevolent smile than a torrent of pathetic words. He carried the sunshine about with him, and in his company men felt that they were in the presence of goodness... There never was a more hard-working bishop, nor one who was more constantly in communication with his clergy. Nor is there a diocese in England where more complete harmony has been maintained. There could be no doubt as to what school in the Church the Bishop belonged to; but his cordiality was so thorough, that no man of a different school remembered it in his presence. His nature was so kindly that it would have pained him exceedingly to have had a difference with one of his clergy.[21]

One newspaper, *The Essex Weekly News*, felt that it had been Wigram's 'private fortune which formed his chief recommendation for the bishopric',* adding it would be a 'great scandal that any diocese should be debarred from having the best possible head that can be found for it, because it entails an expenditure for which the income of the see is inadequate'.[22] However, it seems most unlikely that Wigram had been elevated to the See of Rochester solely for financial reasons: in making his recommendations to Palmerston, the Earl of Shaftesbury's always took into account an individual's faith and pastoral skills, two great assets that Wigram had in large measure.

In sum, it is abundantly clear that Wigram was a remarkable Victorian Christian leader. He was deeply aware of the changing nature of nineteenth-century culture and society. He was greatly concerned over the conditions in which the poor lived and worked and constantly urged the church and his clergy to be active in responding to their needs. He recognised in all of this the cardinal importance of education and promoted it in significant and public ways through his writing, publi-

---

* Wigram left an estate valued at 'under £45,000' (worth around £5 million in 2020 values), see *Aris's Birmingham Gazette*, 25 May 1867.

A Significant Leader

cations and his work as the General Secretary of the National Society. He was strategist, who saw with clarity that the parochial and diocesan structures needed to be overhauled and supplemented. Above all, he was a warm, indeed a delightful outgoing Christian leader with a strong personal faith in Christ, who loved his family and cared for all he met.

Notes

1. J. C. Wigram, *Present Aspects of Popular Education*, 1849, p. 19.
2. J. C. Wigram, *A Charge ... 1860*, p. 5.
3. See Scotland 2000, pp. 70–4, 962, and Heasman 1962, pp. 22–8.
4. *The Essex Weekly News*, 19 April 1867.
5. *The Saturday Review*, 29 December 1860, pp. 829–30.
6. Sumner 1876, p. 397n.
7. *Evangelical Christendom*, 1 May 1867.
8. *The Hertford Mercury and Reformer*, 13 April 1867.
9. Ibid.
10. *The Essex Weekly News*, 12 April 1867.
11. Ibid.
12. *The Herts Guardian, Agricultural Journal, and General Advertiser*, 13 April 1867.
13. *The Saturday Review*, 29 December 1860, p. 829
14. *The Herts Guardian, Agricultural Journal, and General Advertiser*, 13 April 1867.
15. *The Pall Mall Gazette*, 19 January 1867.
16. *The Hertford Mercury and Reformer*, 13 April 1867.
17. Ibid.
18. Ibid.
19. *The Chelmsford Chronicle*, 19 April 1867.
20. Ibid.
21. *The Hertford Mercury and Reformer*, 13 April 1867.
22. *The Essex Weekly News*, 19 April 1867.

Bibliography

Manuscript

Church of England Record Centre, Lambeth Palace
    National Society Archives, Minutes of the General Committee, and Letter Books
Hampshire Record Office
    Parish Registers and Vestry Minutes of the Parish of East Tisted
    J. C. Wigram correspondence as Archdeacon of Winchester
Lambeth Palace Library
    J. C. Wigram correspondence with Archibald Campbell Tait and others.
Southampton City Archives
    Parish records of St Mary's Church, Southampton and Wigram correspondence.
Waltham Forest Archives and Local History Library
    Parish records of St Mary's Church, Leyton
    Manuscript history of Leyton by W. Brenn and J. Kennedy
City of Westminster Archives Centre
    Parish Registers, Vestry Minutes and Church Wardens' Accounts of St James's Church, Piccadilly (Westminster)
    Manuscript history of St Luke's, Berwick Street

Printed: Books and Articles

Anon, *Alumni Oxonienses; the Members of the University of Oxford 1715–1886*.
Anon., *The Rules of the Oxford Society for the Promotion of Gothic Architecture with a List of the Members*. Oxford, 1845.
Arnold, F., *Our Bishops and Deans*. 2 vols. London, Hurst and Blackett, 1875.
Ashwell, A., and R. G. Wilberforce, 1881. *The Life of Samuel Wilberforce*. 3 vols. London: John Murray.
Balleine, G. R., 1933. *A History of the Evangelical Party in the Church of England*. London: Longmans, Green & Co.
Baring-Gould, S., 1914. *The Church Revival*. London: Methuen & Co. Ltd.
Bebbington, D. W., 1989. *Evangelicalism in Modern Britain*. London: Unwin Hyman.
Bell, H. C. F., *Lord Palmerston*. London: Longmans, Green & Co., 1936.

Joseph Cotton Wigram

Benson, A. C., and Viscount Esher (eds), *The Letters of Queen Victoria 1837–1861*. London: John Murray, vol. 3, 1908.

Best, G. F. A., 'The Evangelicals and the Established Church in the Early Nineteenth Century', *Journal of Theological Studies*, 10 January 1959, pp. 63–78.

— *Shaftesbury*. London: B. T. Batsford Ltd, 1964.

Blackie, E. M., 1948. *A Dictionary of Church History*. Oxford: A. R. Mowbray & Co. Ltd.

Bradley, I., 1976. *The Call to Seriousness*. London: Jonathan Cape.

Brose, O. J., 1959. *Church and Parliament: The Reshaping of the Church of England 1828–1860*. Stanford, California: Stanford University Press.

Brown, F. K., 1961. *Fathers of the Victorians*. Cambridge University Press.

Burgess, H. J., 1958. *Enterprise in Education*. London: SPCK.

Burgon, J. W., 1888. *Lives of Twelve Good Men*. 2 vols. London: Scribner & Welford.

Burns, A., 1999. *The Diocesan Revival in the Church of England c. 1800–1870*. Oxford: Clarendon Press.

Carpenter, S. C., *Church and People 1789–1889*. London: SPCK, 1933.

Carter, G., 'Prelates and Priests: The English Episcopate and the Evangelical Clergy', *Christianity and History Newsletter* 14, December 1994, pp. 21–42.

Chadwick, O., 1970. *The Victorian Church*, parts 1 and 2. London: A. & C. Black.

Chamberlain, M. E., *Lord Palmerston*. London: G. P. C. Books, 1987.

Colenso, J. W., 1862. *The Pentateuch and Book of Joshua Critically Examined*. London: Longman & Co.

Conybeare, W. J., 1853. 'Church Parties', *The Edinburgh Review*, October 1853, pp. 273–342.

Cornish, F. W., 1910. *The English Church in the Nineteenth Century*, parts I and II. London: MacMillan and Co. Ltd.

Davidson, R. T., and W. Benham 1891. *Life of Archibald Campbell Tait Archbishop of Canterbury*. 2 vols. London: MacMillan and Co.

Davies, J. S., 1883. *A History of Southampton*. Southampton: Gilbert & Co.

Davys, O. W., [1912]. *A Long Life's Journey with Some I met by the Way*. London: Simpkin, Marshall, Hamilton, Kent & Co. Ltd.

Ditchfield, G. M., *The Evangelical Revival*. London: UCL Press, 1998.

Elliot-Binns, L. E., *The Early Evangelicals*. London: Lutterworth Press, 1953.

— *Religion in the Victorian Era*. London: Lutterworth Press, 1964.

Ellis, I., 1960. *Seven against Christ: A Study of Essays and Reviews*. Leiden: E. J. Brill.

Finlayson, G. B. A. M., *The Seventh Earl of Shaftesbury 1801–1885*. London: Eyre Methuen, 1981.

Filton, R. S., 1989. *The Arkwrights, Spinners of Fortune*. Manchester: Manchester University Press.

Bibliography

Greaves, R. W., 1949. 'The Jerusalem Bishopric, 1841', *English Historical Review*, vol. 64, no. 252, pp. 328–52.

— 1958. 'Golightly and Newman, 1824–1845', *Journal of Ecclesiastical History*, vol. 9, no. 2, pp. 209–28.

Hardman, B. E., 'The Evangelical Party in the Church of England 1855–1865'. Ph.D. thesis, University of Cambridge, 1964.

Heasman, K., 1962. *Evangelicals in Action*. London: Geoffrey Bliss.

Hempton, D., 'Evangelicalism and Eschatology', *The Journal of Ecclesiastical History*, 31.2, 1979, pp. 179–93.

Hilton, B., 1991. *The Age of Atonement*. Oxford: Clarendon Press.

Hinchliff, P. B., 1964. *John William Colenso Bishop of Natal*, London: Nelson.

Hodder, E., 1883. *The Life of the Seventh Earl of Shaftesbury K.G.* 3 vols. London: Cassell & Co. Ltd.

House of Commons, *Report from the Select Committee of the House of Commons on the State of Education*, vol. 1, 1834.

— *Report from the Select Committee of the House of Commons on the Education of the Poorer Classes in England and Wales*, vol. 7, 1838.

Hylson-Smith, K., *Evangelicals in the Church of England 1734–1984*. Edinburgh: T. & T. Clark Ltd, 1988.

Jeune, F. C., *The Studies of Oxford Vindicated in a Sermon preached before the University on Act Sunday, June 29th, 1845 by Francis Jeune DCL Master of Pembroke College, and Late Dean of Jersey*. London: Hatchard and Son, 1845.

— *The Throne of Grace: Not a Confessional. A Sermon Preached before the University of Oxford on Sunday, October 18th, 1846*. London: Hatchard and Son, 1846.

— *St Nicholas College Middle Schools: A Correspondence between the Right Rev. J. C. Wigram, D.D., Lord Bishop of Rochester, and the Rev. F. Jeune, D.C.L., Vice-Chancellor of the University of Oxford, and the Rev. Popularis Aura, an impalpable in the diocese of Rochester*. London: J. T. Hayes, 1862.

Leach, J. C. H., *Sparks of Reform*. Oxford: Pembroke College, 1994

Lubbock, B., 1924. *The Blackwall Frigates*. Glasgow: John Brown & Son.

Marsh, P. T., *The Victorian Church in Decline*. London: Routledge & Kegan Paul, 1969.

Martin, M. C., 1995. 'Women and Philanthropy in Walthamstow and Leyton', *The London Journal*, vol. 2, part 19, pp. 119–49.

Mayor, S., 1967. *The Churches and the Labour Movement*. London: Independent Press Ltd.

Morris, J. N., 1992. *Religion and Urban Change*. Cambridge: Boydell Press.

National Society, *Annual Reports*.

Overton, J. H., *The English Church in the Nineteenth Century 1800–1833*. London, Longmans, Green and Co., 1894.

Packer, J. I., 'The Oxford Evangelicals in Theology', in J. S. Reynolds, *The Evangelicals at Oxford 1735–1871*. Oxford: Marcham Manor Press, 1975.

Pollard, A., 'Evangelical Parish Clergy 1820–1840', *Church Quarterly Review* 159, 1958, pp. 387–95.
Proby, W. H. B., *Annals of the Low Church Party*. London: J. T. Hayes, 1888.
Rack, H. D., 1973. 'Domestic Visitation: A Chapter in Early Nineteenth Century Evangelism', *Journal of Ecclesiastical History* 24.4.
Reardon, B. M. G., 1971. *From Coleridge to Gore*. London: Longman.
Russell, G. W. E., 'The Evangelical Influence', in *Collections and Recollections*. London: Thomas Nelson & Sons, 1903.
— *A Short History of the Evangelical Movement*. London: Mowbray & Co., 1915.
Savell, M. L., 1964. *The Church of England in Leyton*. Leyton Public Libraries.
Scotland, N. A. D., *John Bird Sumner: Evangelical Archbishop*. Leominster: Gracewing, 1995.
— 1997. 'Evangelicals, Anglicans and Ritualism in Victorian England, *Churchman* 3.3, pp. 249–65.
— 2000. *Good and Proper Men. Lord Palmerston and the Bench of Bishops*. Cambridge: James Clarke & Co.
— 2004. *Evangelicals in a Revolutionary Age 1789–1901*. Carlisle, Paternoster Press.
Sinclair, J. (ed.), 1839. *Correspondence of the National Society with the Lords of the Treasury and with the Committee on Education*. London: John Murray.
Soloway, R., *Prelates and People*. London: Routledge & Kegan Paul, 1967.
Sumner, G. H., 1876. *Life of Charles Richard Sumner, D.D. Bishop of Winchester*. London: John Murray.
Thompson, D. M. (ed.), 1972. *Nonconformity in the Nineteenth Century*. London: Routledge & Kegan Paul.
Thomson, W., *Aids to Faith*. London: John Murray, 1861.
Toon, P., 1979. *Evangelical Theology 1833–1856. A Response to Tractarianism*. London: Marshall, Morgan & Scott.
Venn, J. S., 1954. *Alumni Cantabrigienses*. Cambridge: Cambridge University Press.
Vidler, A. R., 1961. *The Church in an Age of Revolution*. Harmondsworth: Pelican.
Wigley, J., *The Rise and Fall of the Victorian Sunday*. Manchester: Manchester University Press, 1980
Wigram, A., *Register of the Wigram Family 1743–1913*. Privately published, Hersham House, 1913.
Wigram, J. C., 'The Advent of the Lord the Present Glory of the Church', in W. Wilson (ed.), *The Blessing of the Lord's Second Advent: Six Lectures During Lent*. London, 1851.
— *A Charge delivered to the Clergy and Churchwardens of the Archdeaconry of Winchester, at his First General Visitation in June, 1848*. London: Operative Jewish Converts' Institution, 1848.
— *A Charge delivered to the Clergy and Churchwardens of the Archdeaconry of Winchester, at his Third General Visitation in April, 1850*. London: Operative Jewish Converts' Institution, 1850.

Bibliography

— *A Charge delivered to the Clergy and Churchwardens of the Archdeaconry of Winchester at his Eighth General Visitation in April, 1855*. London: Operative Jewish Converts' Institution, 1856.

— *A Charge delivered at the Primary Visitation in November, 1860, by Joseph Cotton Wigram, D.D., Bishop of Rochester*. London: Varty, 1860.

— *A Charge Delivered to the Clergy and Churchwardens of the Diocese of Rochester ... in November 1864*. London: Rivington, 1864.

— *The Cottager's Daily Family Prayers*. Chelmsford: T. B. Arthy, 1862.

— *Elementary Arithmetic, Designed for the Information of the Masters and Mistresses of National Schools*. London: J. G. and F. Rivington, 1832.

— *The Geography of the Holy Land intended to serve as an Explanatory key to the Map of Palestine: with a copious index*. London: Roake and Varity, 1832.

— *How to Preach in our Ordinary Congregations: a Charge, delivered to the clergy of the Archdeaconry of Winchester, at his Twelfth General Visitation in April, 1859*. London: Varty, 1859.

— *Helps for the Pastoral Care of St Mary's Southampton*. Southampton, Hott Printers, 1851. Southampton City Archives, MS PR5/7/54.

— *On Humility in the Hour of Success A Sermon Preached on Trinity Sunday June 11th, 1827, by the Rev. Joseph Cotton Wigram MA Domestic Chaplain to his Royal Highness, the Duke of Clarence, Curate of St James Westminster and Secretary to the National Society*. London: C. & J. Rivington, 1827.

— *The Jews. The Appointed Witnesses for God in Successive Ages in the World*. London: published at the request of The London Society for the Promoting of Christianity among the Jews, 1855.

— *A Jubilee Retrospect. Five Sermons on the Progress of the Gospel of Our Lord Jesus Christ Illustrative of the Labours of the Church Missionary Society*. London: Wertheim & Macintosh, 1849.

— *A Letter on the Spiritual Necessities of Portsea Within and Without the Walls addressed to the Principal Inhabitants of the Town and Vicinity*. London: The Operative Jewish Converts' Institution, 1851.

— *A Letter on Sunday School Proceedings in the County of Southampton*. London: Adams and King Printers, 1857.

— *Ministerial Watchfulness. A Sermon Preached at the Visitation of the Rt Revd the Lord Bishop of Winchester in the parish church of Alton on Friday October 17th, 1845*. London: Francis & John Rivington, 1845.

— *Practical Hints on the Formation and Management of Sunday-Schools by The Rev. J. C. Wigram MA Secretary to the National Society for Promoting the Education of the Poor*. London: John W. Parker, 1833.

— *Present Aspects of Popular Education. A Charge delivered to the Clergy and Churchwardens of the Archdeaconry of Winchester at His Second General Visitation in April, 1849*. London: Francis and John Rivington, 1849.

— *St. Nicholas College Middle Schools: A Correspondence between the Right Rev.*

Joseph Cotton Wigram

J. C. Wigram, D.D., Lord Bishop of Rochester, and the Rev. F. Jeune, D.C.L., Vice-Chancellor of the University of Oxford, and the Rev. Popularis Aura, an impalpable in the Diocese of Rochester. London: J. T. Hayes, 1862.
— 'St Paul before Agrippa', in SPCK's *Original Family Sermons*, vol. 1. London: John W. Parker, 1833.
Wigram, R. S., *Biographical Notes Relating to Certain Members of the Wigram Family*. Privately printed by Aberdeen University Press, 1912.
Wilson, H. B. (ed.), 1860. *Essays and Reviews*. London: J. W. Parker & Son.
Wolfe, J., 1991. *The Protestant Crusade in Great Britain 1829–1860*. Oxford: Clarendon Press.
Yates, N., 1983. 'The Anglican Revival in Victorian Portsmouth', in *The Portsmouth Papers*, 37. Portsmouth City Council.

Newspapers

The Atlas
Aris's Birmingham Gazette
The Christian Observer
The Derby and Chesterfield Reporter
The Derby Mercury
The Essex Standard
Evangelical Christendom
The Freeman
The Hampshire Advertiser
The Hampshire Chronicle, Southampton and Isle of Wight Courier
Hertford Mercury and Reformer
The Kentish Gazette
The Kentish Observer
The London Gazette
Norfolk News
The Record
The Rochester, Chatham and Strood Gazette and County Advertiser
The Saturday Review
The Sherborne Mercury (Western Flying Post)
The Southampton and Isle of Wight Courier
The Western-Super-Mare Gazette

Index

Additional Curates' Aid Society 38, 72
Ady, Revd William Brice, Archdeacon of Colchester 67
Allen, Dr 1n.
allotments on glebe land 44
Alton, Hants, address to diocesan clergy 31
Anglo-Catholics 37; see also Roman Catholicism
Arkwright, Anne 11
Arkwright, Revd Joseph 11
Arkwright, Peter 11
Arkwright, Sir Richard 11
Arkwright, Susan Maria see Wigram, Susan Maria
Armstrong, Revd A. 118
Articles of Religion 88, 128
Ashley, Lord, see Shaftesbury, Earl of
atonement 129

Bangor, Bishop of (Christopher Bethell) 20, 23
Bank of Small Deposits 44
banks 70, 76
baptism 8, 29–30, 69, 74
Baptists 92
Baptist Union 92
Barton Stacey, Hants (churchwardens) 32
Baylee, Revd Dr Joseph 93
beards and facial hair, discouraged 73, 110, 111, 134, 145
Bebbington, David 57
Benefit Societies 3, 33
Biblical authority 88, 90–3 *passim*, 94, 96, 127–8, 129, 135, 136
Bickersteth, Revd Edward 106
Bickersteth, Robert, Bishop of Ripon 132

Bird, Charles 106
Birkenhead, St Aidan's College 93
Blackwall ship-building yard, Poplar 1
Blomfield, Charles James, Bishop of London 10, 106, 122
Bonham, Mr (Consul in Naples) 119
'book hawking' 68
book sellers and distributors in Hants 52
Book of Common Prayer 100–1
Booth, General William 139
Bowman, Mr 50
Bradford, John (1510–55) 29
Bradley, Ian 134
Bradwell-on-Sea, Essex (deanery) 66
British and Foreign Bible Society 23, 135, 136
Broadchalke, Hants (living) 89
Broadhurst, Catherine 1n.
Browne, Prof. Harold, Bishop of Ely then Winchester 103, 113, 123
Browne, J. H., Archdeacon 106
Browne, Revd Murray 8
Buckworth-Bailey, Michael 118
Bull, George (1634–1710), Bishop of Llandaff 28
Bunsen, Baron Chevalier Christian Karl 90, 92
Burney, Revd Charles Parr 67, 76
Burns, Arthur 122

Cadell, Revd H. 115
Cambridge: Holy Trinity Church 4; Jesus College 103; King's College 4; St John's College 94; Trinity College 4, 62, 103; Vice-Chancellor of 103

Canterbury, Archbishop of 11 (Manners-Sutton), 88 (Temple); *see also* Sumner, John Bird
Central Protestant Institute 105
Chalk, James 48
Chancellor of the Exchequer 18 (Thomas Spring Rice), 21
Chatham 76; races (opposed) 110
Chelmsford 69, 75, 114; diocese 113; St Mary's 147
Chester, Bishop of *see* Sumner, John Bird
Chichester, Bishop of (Ashurst Gilbert) 106
cholera outbreaks 9 (London), 43–4 (Southampton)
Chrishall, Essex, proposed national school 22–3, 79, 80
church building and repairs 3, 5, 16, 30, 32, 36–7, 38, 44, 49, 50, 73–4, 82
Church Building Societies 3, 72, 135
Church of England Primary Schools 17
Church Missionary Society (CMS) 4, 71, 72, 135, 136; Ladies' Auxiliary 3
Church Pastoral Aid Society 38
church rates 7, 30–1, 46, 49–50
Clarence, H.R.H. the Duke of 7
clergy, the 110–11; working with laity 68–73, *see also* conferences
Clifford, Mary 1n.
Close, Revd Francis 19
Clowes, Major George 120, 146
Colchester 65, 76, 114, 142; Archdeacon of 67; 'Camp Church' 65, 114; St James's 76; St Peter's 115
Colenso, John William, Bishop of Natal 67, 94–9, 110; banned from officiating in Rochester diocese 97, 99
'colloquial intercourse' 28–9
communion *see* Holy Communion

conferences (of clergy and laity) 69, 75, 81, 88, 115, 143
confession 101, 103, 104–5
confirmation 33, 45, 74, 114–16, 142, 144, 145
Conybeare, W. J. 135
Corfu 118
Cottager's Daily Family Prayers (1862) 77–8
Cotton, Joseph 2
Cotton, William 3, 5
Cowper, Lady Emily 61
cricket, clergy discouraged from playing 73, 110, 134, 145
Crowdy, Revd A. 65
Crowther, Revd J. Bryan 118
Cuddesdon College 104
'cult of conduct' 134

Danbury Palace (formerly Place), Essex viii, 64, 79, 97, 104, 111, 118, 120–1, 145
Darwin, Charles 87
Davies, Revd George 73
Davys, Canon O.W. 111, 116
Dengie, Essex (deanery) 66
diocesan administration 81–2
diocesan reform and revival 122, 123
diocesan strategy 66–7
dissenters 18, 22, 46, 79, 80; *see also* nonconformists
Dusautory, H. (churchwarden) 50

Earl's Colne church, Essex (re-opening) 122
East India Company 1, 1n., 4
East India Docks Company 1
East Tisted, Hants 27–39 *passim*, 142; rectory 23, 27; vestry meetings 304
Ebury, Lord 69
Ecclesiastical Commissioners 45
Education: Boards of (diocesan) 19, 52, 55; Committee of the Privy

Index

Council 22, 23, 79, 80; Select Committees on 9, 16–18; *see also* Evangelism; middle classes; National Society; the poor; schools; *and under* Rochester *and* Wigram, Joseph Cotton
Elementary Arithmetic (1832) 12
Ely, Bishop of (Bowyer Sparke) 4; *see also* Browne, J. H.
English Church Union (ECU) 104–5
entertainments/pastimes/recreations (cards, dancing, opera, theatre), discouraged 62, 73, 110, 134
eschatology and the return of Christ 131–3
Escott, Alice (housekeeper) 2
Essays and Reviews (1860) 88–94; Wigram's response to 92–4
Eton College 4, 103
Evangelicalism 57; Wigram's 4, 13, 27, 31, 88, 94, 110, 122, 127–37, 145
Evangelical Revival 4
Evangelicals 13, 20, 37–8, 110, 127, 131, 132, 133, 134, 135, 146; old evangelicals (moderates) 135–6; Recordites (extremists) 135–6
Evangelism in education 16, 22

Faber, George S. 106
farm labourers 13, 27, 80, 122
farmers (take offence) 73
fellowship with the flock essential to true pastoral tradition 68
field sports (hunting, shooting), disapproved 73, 110
Fox, T. 49–50

General Society for Promoting District Visiting 9
Geography of the Holy Land (1832) 12–13, 56, 140
Gladstone, W. E. 19, 102

Golightly, Revd Charles Pourtales 103–4, 105–6
Goode, William 106
Goodman, Mr 44
Goodwin, Charles (Egyptologist) 89, 91
Gospel, The 131
Gravesend, 76, 93; infirmary 66; St George's (sermon at) 64–5
Gray, Robert, Bishop of Cape Town 96
Greaves, R. W. 104

Hampshire Church School(s) Society 53–5
Harper, Edward 105
harvest celebrations 82, 110, 143
Headington, St Andrew's 104
Heathcote, Sir William 56
Hell 133
Herbert, George (1593–1633) 28
Hertford: All Saints' (sermon at) 78; St Andrew's 118
Hertfordshire Board of Education 78
Hervey, Revd Lord Charles 120n.
Heurtley, Charles A. 106
Hilton, Boyd 135
Hinds, Samuel 122
Hoadly Charity 49
Hockerill, Herts, Rochester Diocese Training College 80, 141
Holy Communion (Lord's Supper/table) 29, 30, 74, 100, 101, 117
Holy Spirit, the 129
horse racing 62, 110, 134
House of Lords, Wigram's only speech 22, 79
Howley, William, Bishop of London 4, 7, 10, 122
Huldart's Rope Works 1

Incorporated Church Building Society 72

Joseph Cotton Wigram

Jackson, William, Bishop of Antigua 63
Jerusalem 13, 75; Anglican bishopric of 133; in the 'last days' 131–3 *passim*
Jeune, Francis, Vice-Chancellor of Oxford University 102–3, 104, 105, 106, 108 n.66
Jews and the millennium 13, 56, 131–2, 135
Jones, Revd Francis 117
Jowett, Professor Benjamin 89, 91
Joynes, Revd Richard 65
judgment and the final state 133–4

Kay, Dr J. P. 22
Kenyon, Lord (2nd Baron) 20
King, Revd Brian 145
King's College, London 19, 67, 69, 98, 114, 117–18
Knapp, Revd John 38–9

labouring classes 34, 50, 56, 75, 82
laity, involvement of in parochial work 45, 70, 76, 82, 130, 143; *see also* conferences; scripture readers *and* women
Lambeth, St Mary's 63
Lampeter, St David's College 89
Landport, Hants, circus church 39
Laprimaudaye, Revd Charles Henry 4–5, 5n.
Laprimaudaye, Revd Charles John 5n.
Latton, Essex, church 121, 146; Mark Hall 121
Leeds 46
Letter on the Spiritual Necessities of Portsea 34, 141
Leyton, Essex, St Mary's 5, 5n., 139
Leytonstone, Essex 4–5, 139; new chapel/St John's church 5
libraries 9, 10, 44, 143
Lincoln, Bishop of 20 (John Kaye), 79 (John Jackson)
Lindsay, Colin 104, 105
Lingham, Revd J. F. 63
Llandaff, Bishop of (Alfred Olivant) 23, 79; *see also* Bull, George
London, Bishop of *see* Blomfield; Howley; Porteous; Tait
London and Westminster: College of Advocates 63; Chapel Royal, St James's 144; Exeter Hall 39; Grosvenor Square 144; Montague Place, Marylebone 64; National Society' Training School 16–17; St Helen's, Bishopsgate 2; St James's, Piccadilly, church and parish 5, 7–12 *passim*, 23; St Luke's (chapel-of-ease), Berwick Street 7–12 *passim*, 139; St Mary-le-Bow, Cheapside 63; *see also* King's College; Lambeth *and* Stepney
London Diocesan Church Building Society 3
Lonsdale, John 51
Lord's Day (Sabbath Day) observance 9, 22, 39, 110, 134
Lord's Supper *see* Holy Communion

McCaul, Revd Joseph B. 67, 98
M'Ghie, Revd J. P. 38
Maldon, Essex 75
Manning, Henry 19
Marsden, Samuel 71
Martin, Revd John 39
Medway, River 76
Methodists and Methodism 75, 92, 112, 127
middle classes (education of) 56, 102, 104
Midwinter, Revd N. 54, 55
Mildmay, Carew St John, Archdeacon of Essex 109, 147
millennium/millennialism 13, 87, 132, 135–6

Index

Ministerial Watchfulness (1845) 31
Mission to Seamen Afloat (Medway Branch) 76
missionary work abroad 71, 72, 87; *see also* Church Missionary Society
Mitchell, Revd Mr (school inspector) 53
Model Schools 21, 140
Murray, George, Bishop of Rochester 57, 62

Naples 119–20
National Schools 12, 16 (number of), 17–18, 21, 22, 27, 30, 44–5, 53, 141
National Society for Promoting the Education of the Poor in the Principles of the Established Church 3, 10–11, 12, 16–23, 39, 51–2, 79–80, 140; Central Training School 16–17, 18, 21; Model School 21; Committee of Inquiry and Correspondence 19; Training Institution, Baldwin Gardens 21, 22
nepotism 119
New Barnet church (Lord's Supper administered by a deacon) 117
New Zealand 71, 84 n.46
Newman, John Henry 89, 100, 104
Nicholson, Mr 117
nonconformists 23, 49, 50, 61, 79, 80, 93, 102; *see also* dissenters
Norwich, Bishop of (John Pelham) 103

obituaries and contemporary assessments of Wigram's life and work 145–8
O'Brien, Bishop 106
Operative Jewish Converts' Institution 56, 132
ordination 113–14, 130; candidates' examination topics 113

Owen, Revd L. R. 65
Oxford: Balliol College 89; Christ Church 5n.; Lincoln College 89; 'modern liberalism' in 89; Oriel College 103; Sheldonian Theatre 102–3; Bishop of *see* Wilberforce, Samuel; Vice-Chancellor of *see* Jeune, Francis
Oxford Ecclesiastical Society 32
Oxford Movement 99–100, 130
Oxford Society for the Study of Gothic Architecture 5n.

Palmerston, Lord xi, 61, 94, 109, 122, 123, 142, 148
parishes: division of 8, 44, 46–7, 48, 141; parochial system 36, 46, 141
Pattison, Mark 89, 91
Pearce, Nanny 2
pew rents 37, 39
Pitt, William (Prime Minister) 2
Pitt Club 2
Pius IX, Pope 102
poor, the: educational needs of 11–12, 14, 51, 139, 141; free seats in church for 34, 37, 39; a gospel for 75–8; Wigram's concern for 14, 29, 64, 75–7 *passim*, 82, 142, 148
Porteous, Beilby, Bishop of London 5
Portsea, Hants 34–9, 109, 141; All Saints 35, 36, 38; beer shops and public houses 35, 37; new churches (proposed) 35–7; population 34–5; St George's 35, 37; St John's 35, 37, 38–9; St Mary's 34, 35; St Paul's 35, 38; social conditions in 34–5; vicar of (obstructive) 37–8
Portsmouth, Hants 36, 37, 141; free church seats 37; population 37; St Luke's 39; St Simon's 39; St Thomas's 33; social conditions 109; *see also* Landport *and* Portsea

Powell, Professor Baden 89, 90
Practical Hints on the Formation and Management of Sunday-Schools (1833) 13–14, 140
preachers/preaching (qualities needed) 111–13
Present Aspects of Education (1849) 140
Prittlewell, Essex (Wigram's nephew appointed to living) 119
Privy Council, Education Committee of 22, 23, 79, 80
Protestantism, Wigram's 88, 102, 128, 134
Provident Institutions and Societies 9, 43, 70, 76
Pugh, Mr (chaplain at Naples) 119

Queen Victoria 63

Ragged Schools 135
railways (trains) viii–ix, 43, 65, 110
rates *see* church rates
Recordites 135–6
Redesdale, Lord (later Earl of) 23, 79
Reid's Brewery 1
religious census (1851) 46, 87
Richerius (11th-century priest) 43
ritualism 99–106, 110, 145
Rochester 93; Cathedral 62, 63–4 (Wigram's enthronement), 98, 114, 116, 129; diocese, history and extent of viii, 64, 122–3; educational needs of diocese 78–81; St Nicholas's (sermon in) 63
Rockford House, Cromford, Derbyshire 11
Roman Catholicism: restoration of hierarchy 101; rites imitated by Anglicans 88, 101
Romford, Essex, St Edward's (confirmation at) 114–15
Rotherfield, Hants, Scott family home 27
Round, Charles G. (farmer) 73
Royal South Hampshire Hospital 44
rural deans 52, 66–8 *passim*, 81, 93, 110, 117, 129, 143
Russell, Lord John 16, 17
Ryder, Dudley and Mrs 116

Sabbath observance *see* Lord's Day
sacraments 74
sailors 34, 76, 142; home for in Poplar 1–2
St Albans, Herts: Abbey 115, 123; diocese 123
St Nicholas College, Shoreham 103, 105, 108 n.66
Sanitary Condition, etc., of the Borough of Portsmouth, including the Isle of Portsea 109
Schools *see* Church of England Primary; Hampshire Church; Model; National; Ragged; Sunday; Woodard
Scotland, Revd John 44
Scott, James W. 27
Scott, Revd T. 95
Scripture readers 44, 45, 46, 68
Select Committees of the House of Commons on Education *see* Education, Select Committees
Shaftesbury, 7th Earl of (styled Lord Ashley until 1851) 19, 39, 46, 61, 122, 132, 142, 148; wife of (Minnie) 61
Shaw, Revd R. W. 66
Sheepshanks, John, Bishop of Columbia 122
Simeon, Revd Charles 4, 67
Sinclair, Revd John 20
slave trade 135
smoking, discouraged 73
Snooke, Revd H. 38
Society for the Promotion of Christian Knowledge 12

Index

Society for the Propagation of the Gospel in Foreign Parts (SPG) 3, 55–6, 71, 72
soldiers 34 (wives), 65, 76, 114, 142,
South Stoneham, rectory 44
South West Bible Society Auxiliary 3
Southampton 43–55, 109, 142; All Saints 48–9; Bernard Street district 44, 47; Freemantle district 43; insanitary conditions 43; National School site, Chapel Road 50; National Schools, Grove Street 44, 45; Newtown district 43, 44, 47; Northam district 43, 44, 47; parish structure and re-organisation 46–51; Royal South Hampshire Hospital 44; St Mary's 39, 43, 44, 45, 47, 50, 57, 114, 141; store rooms used for worship and a school 48; Wigram's strategy for 45–6; Young Men's Library and Reading Room 44
Southampton Common 51
SPCK 14, 15, 52
sports (archery, rifle shooting) clergy discouraged from participating in 73; *see also* cricket *and* field sports
Stanley, Arthur, later Dean of Westminster 89
Stepney, chapel/new church (St Philip's) 3
Stewart, Revd C. 38
Stewart, Revd J. V. 37, 38
Strange, Mrs Robert 119
Strood, Kent (re-opening of church) 66
Sumner, Charles Richard, Bishop of Winchester 31–2, 37, 39, 43, 49, 51, 57–8, 63, 111n.
Sumner, John Bird, Bishop of Chester/Archbishop of Canterbury 16, 31, 49, 62, 113

Sunday excursion trains, disapproved of 110
Sunday School Committee (diocesan) 52
Sunday schools 13–14, 15, 51, 52–3, 65, 81, 140; teachers 9, 33, 44, 52, 65, 69, 80
Sutton, Revd G. P. 118

Tait, Archibald Campbell, Bishop of London 96, 104, 116, 117, 118, 120
Tamley, Revd Mr 118
Temple, Frederick 89–90
Tennyson, Alfred Lord 87
Thames, River 8–9 (pollution), 76
Thompson, Revd W. 119
Tract Ninety (XC/90) 89, 92
Tractarians/Tractarianism 99–100, 101, 104–6 *passim*, 135
training for teachers 16–19 *passim*, 21, 33, 44, 80, 93; *see also* National Society *and* Hockerill College
Treasury (Her Majesty's) 16, 20–2, 140

Villiers, Henry Montagu, Bishop 132
Visitations and Charges: archdiaconal 33, 53, 54, 134, 140; diocesan 66, 68, 70, 80, 81, 94, 98, 111, 112, 114, 122, 128, 129, 131, 143
visiting societies (diocesan) 9, 44

Waldron, Revd 117–18
Waltham Abbey 93, 118
Walthamstow church 2
Walthamstow Female Benefit Society 3
Walthamstow House, Essex 1, 2
Walwood House, Leytonstone 5
Ward, Revd John Gifford 7, 8, 23 n.1
Warleigh, Revd A. J. 118–19
Waterside Mission, Gravesend 76
Watson, Revd J. 119
Watson, Revd W. 116–17

Joseph Cotton Wigram

Westminster *see* London
Wexford, Ireland 1n., 2
Wheathampton, Herts 111
Wigram, Alfred 57
Wigram, Anne 11
Wigram, Arthur Henry 120, 125 n.53
Wigram (*née* Watts), Eleanor, Lady Wigram 1, 2, 3, 10–11, 71
Wigram, Eustace Rochester 121
Wigram, Sir James 11
Wigram, John 1n.
Wigram, Joseph Cotton
  birth 1; baptism 2; education 3–4; ordained 3; marriage 11; children 11, 19, 57, 120, 121; family life 120–2; private fortune 148; death 144; funeral 146; *see also* obituaries
  appointments: curate of Leytonstone 3; assistant preacher/curate St James's, Piccadilly 5; Secretary to National Society 11, resignation 19–20; Rector of East Tisted 23; Archdeacon of Winchester 31; Rector of St Mary's Southampton 39, 43; Bishop of Rochester 61–3
  arms (heraldic) at Trinity College, Cambridge 62
  character and personal qualities 58, 111, 134, 136, 144; 'a bishop of little things' 110, 144; personal religion 127; tributes to 20, 54–5
  education: devotion to 22, 33, 51, 54, 56, 65, 78–82 *passim*, 139, 142, 148; Christian basis essential 17, 18, 21, 81, 140; evidence to Select Committee 16–18; opposed to government secularisation of 19, 21–2, 80, 100, 140
  engagement schedules (in 1861) 67 (clergy conferences), 115–16 (confirmations)
  sermons preached 7, 31, 56, 57, 64, 65, 66, 71, 72, 77, 78, 84 n.46, 129, 131–2, 136
Wigram, Sir Robert 1, 1n., 2, 3, 10
Wigram, Revd Spencer (nephew) 115, 119
Wigram, Susan Caroline 11
Wigram (*née* Arkwright), Susan Maria 11, 120n., 121
Wigram, Walter 57
Wilberforce, Samuel, Bishop of Oxford xi, 104, 106
Wilkinson, Joseph (scripture reader) 45–6
Williams, Professor Rowland 89, 90, 92
Wilson, Revd Henry Bristow 89, 90–1
Winchester 51, 52, 53, 54, 71; Bishop of *see* Sumner, Charles Richard; Archdeacon of (Wigram) 31–9; Dean of (Thomas Garnier) 54; St Lawrence's 32; Winchester College 35, 54
Wirksworth, Derbyshire 11
Wiseman, Cardinal Nicholas, Archbishop of Westminster 102
women (ladies), involvement of in church life 3, 9–10, 45, 70–1, 75, 82, 130, 143
Wood, S. F. 19
Woodard, Nathaniel 102, 103
Woodard schools 104; *see also* St Nicholas College
Woodcock, Revd E. 32
'worldly distractions' 134
working classes, special services for 64, 76

Yokohama 118
Young, Arthur 4

www.ingramcontent.com/pod-product-compliance
Lightning Source LLC
Chambersburg PA
CBHW032257150426
43195CB00008BA/485